FOCUS ON THE FAMILY'S

The Truth project

DAILY

TRAVELOGUE

scripture devotional

Dr. Del Tackett *and* Jim Ware

Designed by Brian Gage Design
Edited by Grant Cheney

Printed in the United States of America
1 2 3 4 5 6 7 8 9 / 13 12 11 10 09 08 07

ISBN-10: 1-58997-530-8
ISBN-13: 978-1-58997-530-9

Do not conform any longer to the

pattern of this world, but be transformed

by the renewing of your mind.

Romans 12:2 (NIV)

Contents

Contents

I am excited that you have chosen to invest your time in *Focus on the Family's The Truth Project®*. The Lord appears to be blessing this program on a global scale – participants around the globe report that He is using this curriculum to expand their understanding of biblical truth and deepen their spiritual walk. I pray He uses it to do the same for you. I'm also thankful that you have decided to spend a little time each day reflecting upon God's truth claims as we visit them together on our tours. It's my earnest desire that your time and effort will pay rich dividends, not only in the way of enhancing your weekly study, but also by drawing you into a closer relationship with the Lord.

The highest and most glorious privilege given to mankind is the offer God extends to His children to draw near to Him. It is amazing – and crushingly disturbing – that we so often neglect that unbelievable invitation. Jesus said, "Behold, I stand at the door and knock. If anyone hears My voice and opens the door, I will come in to him and dine with him, and he with Me" (Revelation 3:20). Who would ever pass up a chance to have dinner with Jesus? Sadly, we do it all the time.

The staff of *The Truth Project* wants to see that change. Ultimately, we long for the Body of Christ to become strong and healthy, with a growing, vibrant, and authentic relationship with the Lord – the kind of relationship we see illustrated in the life of David.

One cannot read the Psalms without being struck by the closeness and yet complete openness of David's interaction with God. There is nothing clinical about this relationship. There is no posturing, no pretending – just genuine communion and a stark acknowledgment of what is really real. David consistently confesses the truth of who God is and who man is. He's not afraid to admit his own shortcomings. He understands that when one contemplates the greatness of God, the exercise often raises pesky questions. That's because the bright light of Truth has an uncomfortable way of exposing the lies, distortions, and pathologies that lie hidden within the human heart.

Our desire in putting together this scripture devotional is to provide you with a springboard to this kind of open, honest, and nitty-gritty contemplation of God and self. As you go through *The Truth Project* weekly lessons, these daily reflections are designed to draw you closer to Him, His Truth, and the healthy self-examination that naturally comes from gazing upon His face.

You will notice that this devotional contains thirteen chapters that correspond directly with the thirteen tours of *The Truth Project* DVD curriculum. Each chapter contains seven days of reflection to help keep key Scripture in the forefront of your mind throughout the week. You may choose to use the *Daily Travelogue* in conjunction with the video series or you may decided to use the devotional after completing the video series as ongoing study into the Scripture. However you chose to use it, we are confident the Lord will bless your time contemplating His majesty.

Each day you will find the following:

A list of passages from God's Word.

I enjoin you to read these Scriptures carefully and prayerfully. Contemplate what they reveal about God's nature and what they reveal about man. This is offered merely as a stimulus to your own meditations upon God's Truth.

A question that will hopefully aid you in self-examination.

This is not meant to depress you but to help you follow the Psalmist's lead in recognizing and confessing your shortcomings before the grandeur and goodness of God.

A place for you to record your thoughts.

For those who may never have done this, I would encourage you to give it a try. Writing both stimulates and clarifies our thinking. You may be surprised at what you find flowing from your pen!

A short prayer.

This, too, is intended simply as a starter for your own conversation with the Lord, which should include praise, adoration, confession, thanksgiving, and petition.

It has been my experience that whenever I invest time in developing my relationship with the Lord, He overwhelms me with increased blessings and manifestations of His presence. Amazing, isn't it? It makes me wonder why we neglect so great a privilege. He has given us an open invitation, and the benefits of accepting are infinitely rewarding.

Our fervent prayer has been that God would do His deep transformational work within the hearts of all those who go through *The Truth Project*. If this short devotional guide can be of help to you in that process of transformation, then the effort to create it will have been of immense worth. May the Lord bless you and draw you ever closer to Himself.

soli deo gloria!

*P.S. One final note of encouragement. Most of our lives are full and sometimes very hectic. The chances are high that you are going to miss a day or two … or three. When you do, there will be a little whisper in your ear telling you to quit because you are somehow "behind." Don't listen to it. You will **never** be behind! Just jump back in on the current day and keep going. The Lord loves perseverance … because **He** perseveres with us.*

Conduct yourselves with wisdom toward

outsiders, making the most of the opportunity.

Let your speech always be with grace, as though

seasoned with salt, so that you will know how

you should respond to each person.

Colossians 4:5-6 (NASB)

"You are a king, then!" said Pilate.

Jesus answered, "You are right in saying I am a king.

In fact, for this reason I was born, and for this

I came into the world, to testify to the truth.

Everyone on the side of truth listens to me."

"What is truth?" Pilate asked.

John 18:37-38 (NIV)

tour **1**

Veritology

what is **Truth**?

ἐγὼ εἰς τοῦτο
γεγέννημαι καὶ εἰς τοῦτο
ἐλήλυθα εἰς τὸν κόσμον,
ἵνα μαρτυρήσω τῇ
ἀληθείᾳ

THE CENTRALITY OF TRUTH

Pilate therefore said to Him, "Are You a king then?"
Jesus answered, "You say rightly that I am a king. For
this cause I was born, and for this cause I have come
into the world, that I should bear witness to the truth.
Everyone who is of the truth hears My voice."
Pilate said to Him, "What is truth?"
John 18:37, 38, NKJV

Justice is turned back, and righteousness stands afar
off; for truth is fallen in the street, and equity
cannot enter. So truth fails, and he who departs
from evil makes himself a prey.
Isaiah 59:14, 15, NKJV

"What is truth?" Pilate doesn't seem to have grasped the importance of his ironic question. Without the plumb line of Truth, we can know neither life, goodness, righteousness, nor justice. We can't even know ourselves. This is why Jesus, the King of all creation, came into the world *to serve and bear witness to the Truth.*

What would it mean to live in a world without Truth? Have I pondered the immensity of Pilate's question?

question

response

prayer

Lord, open my eyes and grant me a vision of the devastating emptiness of a life lived apart from any reliable standard of goodness and reality. Help me to grapple with the precepts of Your Word, that I may order my life around the nucleus of the living Christ. Grant me compassion for those who are strangers to Your Truth. I thank You for Your guiding presence in my life.

THE SUBSTANCE OF TRUTH

Jesus said to him, "I am the way, the truth, and the life.
No one comes to the Father except through Me."
John 14:6, NKJV

...Attaining to all riches of the full assurance of
understanding, to the knowledge of the mystery
of God, both of the Father and of Christ, in whom
are hidden all the treasures of wisdom and
knowledge ... For in Him dwells all the fullness
of the Godhead bodily ...
Colossians 2:2, 3, 9, NKJV

Biblically speaking, Truth is both *relational* and *propositional*. It is at
one and the same time a *Person* – Jesus Christ, God in the flesh – *and*
a set of verbally expressible, mentally comprehensible statements *about*
that Person and the invisible God He reveals. This Truth is consistent
with reality: it matches the observable facts of the universe while
simultaneously explaining realities we cannot see. In this way, it integrates
all knowledge and experience into a meaningful whole.

Do I consistently turn to the Source of Truth for answers to my questions?

question

---

response

---

prayer

You alone, Father, are the fountain of Truth. All things are weighed and measured against the standard of **Your** nature and character. Let this simple but profound realization permeate all my thoughts and perceptions. Enable me to look upon Your face and see reflections of Your glory in every nook and cranny of the world You have created.

TRUTH AND FAITH

Therefore know this day, and consider it in your heart,
that the LORD Himself is God in heaven above and on
the earth beneath; there is no other.
Deuteronomy 4:39, NKJV

Now faith is the substance of things hoped for,
the evidence of things not seen.
Hebrews 11:1, NKJV

But He said to them, "Why are you fearful,
O you of little faith?"
Matthew 8:26, NKJV

There's a tendency in our day to separate "reality" from "spirituality." It's part of the innate human propensity for compartmentalizing knowledge, belief, and behavior – in other words, for **hypocrisy**. Biblical Truth demands a **total** response. It elicits **action** as well as mental assent. If I believe that what I believe is really real, I will step out and act upon it. This is the meaning of the biblical word *faith*.

Do my actions reflect or deny my spoken beliefs?

Unite my heart to fear Your name, O Lord (Psalm 86:11). Let the words of my mouth and the meditations of my heart be acceptable in Your sight (Psalm 19:14). Give me faith, not merely in faith alone, but in the solid reality of Truth – the Truth **You** embody and declare to the world.

THE WATERSHED OF TRUTH

"Do not think that I came to bring peace on earth.
I did not come to bring peace but a sword."
Matthew 10:34, NKJV

"But because I tell the truth, you do not believe Me."
John 8:45, NKJV

The light of Christ disperses the darkness of the devil's lies. But in so doing, it splits human society and draws a line through the center of every human heart. In a fallen world – a world divided into warring camps – the Truth gains enemies simply by *being true*.

Does this concept frighten me into hiding, feigning, or running away?

question

---

response

---

prayer

Search me, O God, and know my heart; try me, and know
my anxieties; and see if there is any wicked way in me (Psalm
139:23). Show me where I stand in relation to the dividing chasm.
Subject my attitudes and actions to the pruning blade of your
absolute Truth. Take away my tendency to flinch from the bright
sharpness of its all-revealing light.

TAKING CAPTIVITY CAPTIVE

He feeds on ashes; a deceived heart has turned him aside; and he cannot deliver his soul, nor say, "Is there not a lie in my right hand?"
Isaiah 44:20, NKJV

A servant of the Lord must not quarrel but be gentle to all, able to teach, patient, in humility correcting those who are in opposition, if God perhaps will grant them repentance, so that they may know the truth, and that they may come to their senses and escape the snare of the devil, having been taken captive by him to do his will.
2 Timothy 2:24-26, NKJV

Those who have been ensnared by Satan's ruse – those who stand on the far side of the chasm – are not in a position to free themselves from the darkness of deception. They don't see the lie they are holding in their hand. Captives can seldom be liberated by means of a simplistic approach. This is a task that requires wisdom, humility, and a commitment to prayer. A winsome attitude and a genuine heart of love are prerequisites for effectively wielding the sword of Truth.

Is this my approach to outsiders?

question

_____

_____

_____

_____

_____

response

_____

_____

Thank You, God, for delivering me from the power of darkness and conveying me into the kingdom of Your Son (Colossians 1:13). I praise You for the gifts of repentance and faith. Lead me today to someone who stands in desperate need of the same kind of deliverance. Help me to show that person Your grace and goodness in such a way that he or she will be drawn into the circle of Your Truth.

THINKING AND BEING

As he thinks in his heart, so is he ...
Proverbs 23:7, NKJV

And do not be conformed to this world, but
be transformed by the renewing of your mind,
that you may prove what is that good and
acceptable and perfect will of God.
Romans 12:2, NKJV

It's often been said that you are what you eat. Where the life of the
heart and the mind are concerned, the ruling principle is "You are what
you *think*." That's why *thinking rightly* – in harmony with objective,
absolute Truth – is a matter of such critical importance. Your *mindset*
is the root of all you are, the source of everything you do. As the twig is
bent, so grows the tree.

Do I discipline my thoughts, or do I often let them run unchecked?

question

response

prayer

Create in me a clean heart, O God, and renew a steadfast spirit within me (Psalm 51:10). Shed the light of Your Truth upon the inner workings of my mind. Show me how mental habits and patterns of thought impact my relationship with You and color my perception of the reality in which You have called me to live. I thank You, for I know that You will keep him in perfect peace whose mind is stayed on You (Isaiah 26:3).

OPEN OR CLOSED?

They confronted me in the day of my calamity, but the LORD was my support. He also brought me out into a broad place; He delivered me because He delighted in me.
Psalm 18:18, 19, NKJV

...For all things are yours: whether Paul or Apollos or Cephas, or the world or life or death, or things present or things to come – all are yours. And you are Christ's, and Christ is God's.
1 Corinthians 3:21-23, NKJV

How broad is your outlook on reality? How expansive is your *philosophy* of life? Herein lies one of the sweetest ironies of the Christian worldview: the way to genuine openness and inclusiveness lies through the *narrow gate*. In renouncing all for Jesus' sake, we become heirs to the entire universe. But those who deny God's reality and cling only to the visible world shut themselves up in a box with a tightly closed lid.

Are my thoughts grand or primarily small and self-centered?

_____

_____

_____

_____

_____

_____

_____

You, O Lord, are the God who opens prison doors and sets the captives free. Open my eyes that I might perceive the infinite joys of the reality You have created. Take the lid off my box and lead me out under the expansiveness of Your heavens. Let me see the endless applications and interconnections of Your all-inclusive Truth.

See to it that no one takes you captive through hollow and

deceptive philosophy, which depends on human tradition and

the basic principles of this world rather than on Christ.

Colossians 2:8 (NIV)

tour 2

Philosophy & Ethics

says **Who**?

STAY FREE, LIVE FREE

Beware lest anyone cheat you through philosophy
and empty deceit, according to the tradition of men,
according to the basic principles of the world,
and not according to Christ.
Colossians 2:8, NKJV

... lest Satan should take advantage of us; for
we are not ignorant of his devices.
2 Corinthians 2:11, NKJV

But even if our gospel is veiled, it is veiled to those
who are perishing, whose minds the god of this age
has blinded, who do not believe, lest the light
of the gospel of the glory of Christ, who is the
image of God, should shine on them.
2 Corinthians 4:3, 4, NKJV

In some ways the Cosmic Battle can be reduced to a confrontation between two "gods": Jehovah, the one true God; and Satan, the false "god" of this present age. As sojourners living in enemy territory, under the shadow of the usurper's rule, Christians can all too easily succumb to the influence of *his* perspective on life and reality. That perspective

PHILOSOPHY & ETHICS: says **Who**?

assaults us daily in the form of popular philosophy and contemporary cultural assumptions.

Am I constantly on my guard against the whispered suggestions of a malicious and deceptive Enemy?

Father in heaven, enlighten my eyes. Keep me from sleeping the sleep of death. Let my enemy have no occasion to say, "I have prevailed against him" (Psalm 13:3, 4). Teach me to distrust my own inclinations and to turn away from the seductive messages of the surrounding culture. I choose to lean instead upon the unfailing Truth of Your Word. You have delivered me from the snares of the fowler and from the pestilence that walks in darkness (Psalm 91:3, 6). Set a watch upon my heart (Nehemiah 4:9) and hide me in the shadow of Your secret place (Psalm 91:1).

HOLLOW MEN

...."Well did Isaiah prophesy of you hypocrites,
as it is written: 'This people honors Me with
their lips, but their heart is far from Me. And in vain
they worship Me, teaching as doctrines
the commandments of men.'"
Mark 7:6, 7; Isaiah 29:13, NKJV

For since, in the wisdom of God, the world
through wisdom did not know God, it pleased God
through the foolishness of the message preached
to save those who believe ... Because the foolishness
of God is wiser than men, and the weakness
of God is stronger than men.
1 Corinthians 1:21, 25, NKJV

T. S. Eliot wrote of "The Hollow Men": straw-filled scarecrows with dry voices, leaning together for support in the whispering wind.[1] This is a striking image of the emptiness of merely human wisdom – a void that not even "star stuff" is sufficient to fill. Apart from God, the Source of Truth and the Ground of Being, man's attempts to make sense of his existence fall flat, like a lever without a fulcrum. In Shakespeare's famous phrase, they are like "a tale told by an idiot, full of sound and fury, signifying nothing."

Is my quest for wisdom and knowledge self-oriented, people-oriented, or God-oriented? *question*

response

prayer

Show me Your ways, O Lord; Teach me Your paths. Lead me in Your Truth and teach me, for You are the God of my salvation (Psalm 25:4, 5). I know that there is neither life nor redemption in merely human speculation, just as blindness leaves us groping in the dark. Be my Vision, my Light, and my Truth. Let the so-called folly of the crucified Savior shape and inform my understanding of every aspect of Your world.

---

[1] T. S. Eliot, "The Hollow Man", in *The Book of Living Verse*, ed. Louis Untermeyer (New York: Harcourt, Brace and Company, 1945), 549-552.

THINGS ABOVE

In the beginning God created the heavens and the earth.
Genesis 1:1, NKJV

So it came to pass, at the end of forty days,
that Noah opened the window of the ark ...
Genesis 8:6, NKJV

If then you were raised with Christ, seek those things
which are above, where Christ is, sitting at the right
hand of God. Set your mind on things above, not on
things on the earth.
Colossians 3:1, 2, NKJV

All things have a beginning, just as they must also have an end. But in the beginning God already was, and in the end He will remain the same. Above the heavens, below the earth, beyond the range of the visible and the knowable, His presence extends forever like an endless sea. Our little world floats within the matrix of His Truth like the ark upon the flood. We have only to open a window and look up to become aware of the larger reality that surrounds us.

Does my perspective take into account the invisible truth of heavenly realities? Or is it merely one-dimensional? *question*

response

prayer

Your mercy, O Lord, is in the heavens; your faithfulness reaches to the clouds (Psalm 36:5). Lift my eyes to the everlasting hills. Inspire me moment by moment to keep looking upward, knowing that my redemption draws near in Christ (Luke 21:28). Rescue me from the narrow emptiness of the closed cosmic cube. Be exalted, O God, above the heavens; let Your glory be above all the earth (Psalm 57:11).

THE GOD WHO IS THERE ... **AND** HERE

> You are near, O Lᴏʀᴅ, and all Your
> commandments are truth.
> **Psalm 119:151, NKJV**
>
> "Am I a God near at hand," says the Lᴏʀᴅ, "and not
> a God afar off? Can anyone hide himself in secret
> places, so that I shall not see him?" says the Lᴏʀᴅ;
> "Do I not fill heaven and earth?" says the Lᴏʀᴅ.
> **Jeremiah 23:23, 24, NKJV**
>
> Then she called the name of the Lᴏʀᴅ who spoke
> to her, You-Are-the-God-Who-Sees; for she said,
> "Have I also here seen Him who sees me?"
> **Genesis 16:13, NKJV**

Unlike His creatures, God exists outside the "cosmic cube." But He isn't content to remain there. Instead, He constantly invades our space, lifting the lid of the box, reaching inside, speaking to us, reminding us that we live under the gaze of His watchful eye. Our grasp of life and reality is most profound when we see the "stuff inside the box" in the light of this divinely revealed but intensely personal and immediate Truth.

reflection

What would it be like to live as if God really sees me, knows me, and cares intimately about every detail of my existence? *question*

response

_____

_____

_____

_____

_____

_____

_____

prayer

I thank You, Father, for Your active involvement in my life. It is the ground of all my confidence. Make me ever mindful of Your merciful presence. Teach me to filter my perceptions of life, the world, myself, and other people through the grid of Your inspired Word. Grant me the keys to knowledge, wisdom, and beauty. For it is in Your light alone that we see light (Psalm 36:9).

THE HUB OF THE WHEEL

The craftsman stretches out his rule... He cuts down cedars for himself and takes the cypress and the oak... He burns half of it in the fire... And the rest of it he makes into a god, his carved image. He falls down before it and worships it, prays to it and says, "Deliver me, for you are my god!"
Isaiah 44:13-17, NKJV

For by Him all things were created that are in heaven and that are on earth, visible and invisible, whether thrones or dominions or principalities or powers. All things were created through Him and for Him. And He is before all things, and in Him all things consist.
Colossians 1:16, 17, NKJV

Just as you can't make a real god out of a piece of wood, neither can you construct a true and comprehensive worldview out of the sticks and scraps of random facts and observations. There's a grand pattern to the universe that doesn't fully emerge until we gain access to the master plan. Without the hub, the spokes of the wheel fall apart. In the same way, without Christ at its core, human existence collapses into an absurd pile of disconnected component parts.

question

What does my outlook reveal about the God (or gods) I worship?

response

prayer

Lord Jesus Christ, I confess that You are the Wheel in the Middle of the Wheel (Ezekiel 1:16). All things were made through You, and without You nothing was made that was made (John 1:3). There can be no systematic thinking about the nature of things, no ordered and meaningful perspective on the purpose of life in this world, that does not put You at the center of the picture. Reorient my life around the nucleus of worship. Help me to see You as Lord of every situation.

IMAGES

> Then God said, "Let Us make man in Our image,
> according to Our likeness; let them have dominion
> over the fish of the sea, over the birds of the air, and
> over the cattle, over all the earth and over every
> creeping thing that creeps on the earth."
> **Genesis 1:26, NKJV**
>
> You shall not make for yourself a carved image – any
> likeness of anything that is in heaven above,
> or that is in the earth beneath, or that is in
> the water under the earth...
> **Exodus 20:4, NKJV**
>
> He is the image of the invisible God,
> the firstborn over all creation.
> **Colossians 1:15, NKJV**

The Law of Moses forbade the fabrication of visible images of the invisible God. Why? Because *in mankind God had already given the world a perfectly customized representation of Himself*. This was to be Adam's role within creation's master plan: to stand at the center of the universe as a living picture of the Creator, faithfully reflecting the glory of the One who had made him. The Second Adam, Jesus Christ, redeems this aspect of humanity's purpose and destiny. He raises the fallen image from the dust of death.

"Image of God" or "goo man": What is my concept of human nature, and how does it affect the way I live?

question

response

prayer

Father, grant me a fresh understanding of what it means to be a child of the King, a creature related to the Creator in a unique and unparalleled way. Truly I am Your servant and the son of Your maidservant (Psalm 116:16). I and the children You have given to me are for signs and wonders in Israel from the Lord of hosts, who dwells in Mount Zion (Isaiah 8:18). Teach us to see ourselves as such and to live lives worthy of the vision.

REGRET

What is man that You are mindful of him, and the son of man that You visit him? For You have made him a little lower than the angels, and You have crowned him with glory and honor.
Psalm 8:4, 5, NKJV

Then the LORD saw that the wickedness of man was great in the earth, and that every intent of the thoughts of his heart was only evil continually. And the LORD was sorry that He had made man on the earth, and He was grieved in His heart.
Genesis 6:5, 6, NKJV

What does it mean to be human? Among other things, it means having *regrets*. It means paradox and ambiguity – lost opportunities; shattered dreams; sharp, bittersweet longings. To be a man or a woman is to pass your days as a walking, breathing self-contradiction: crowned with glory and honor, yet twisted through self-obsession and deceit. How can such a stunning creature have fallen to such great depths? How can he or she be restored? These are the defining questions of our existence.

reflection

Do heartfelt remorse and repentance figure significantly in my view of myself and my relationship with God?

question

response

prayer

It is a fearful thing that I have to ask, O Lord, but I ask it all the same: Let me see myself in the mirror of **Your** Truth. Measure me by the standard of **Your** goodness. Reveal to me both the wonder and the horror of my present condition. Show me what it means to be the crippled bearer of the broken divine image. I acknowledge my transgressions and confess that I have been brought forth in iniquity (Psalm 51:5). Let this realization compel me to find refuge in Your grace alone.

So I say, live by the Spirit, and you will not

gratify the desires of the sinful nature. For

the sinful nature desires what is contrary to the Spirit,

and the Spirit what is contrary to the sinful nature.

They are in conflict with each other,

so that you do not do what you want.

Galatians 5:16-17 (NIV)

tour **3**

Anthropology

who is **Man**?

UP AND DOWN

And the Lord God formed man of the dust of the ground, and breathed into his nostrils the breath of life; and man became a living being.
Genesis 2:7, NKJV

As a father pities his children, so the Lord pities those who fear Him. For He knows our frame; He remembers that we are dust.
Psalm 103:13, 14, NKJV

And so it is written, "The first man became a living being." The last Adam became a life-giving spirit.
1 Corinthians 15:45, NKJV

Man is unique among God's creatures. He alone bears the immediate marks of the Creator's shaping hand. Formed, like the plants and animals, of the physical stuff of the ground, he nevertheless lives *spiritually* by direct infusion of the very breath of life, the *ruach* or Spirit of God. His orientation to reality is therefore double-sided: his eyes are turned both upward and downward. To grasp this fundamental truth is to perceive something of the wonder *and* the tension of human experience.

ANTHROPOLOGY: who is **Man**?

In what practical ways is my daily existence impacted by the "upward" and "downward" aspects of my dual human nature?

I understand, Lord, that You have special plans for me. I belong to this world because I am part of it. But I also ache to be at home with You in the heavenly realm (2 Corinthians 5:2; Philippians 1:23), for I bear the stamp of Your divine image as the identifying mark of my humanity. Teach me to negotiate the challenges of this two-sided existence. Deliver me from the temptation to emphasize or exploit one aspect of my God-given nature at the expense of the other. I long to be entirely Yours.

OUT OF KILTER

So God created man in His own image; in the image
of God He created him; male and female he created them.
Genesis 1:27, NKJV

Then to Adam [God] said, "Because you have heeded
the voice of your wife, and have eaten from the tree of
which I commanded you, saying, 'You shall not eat of it':
Cursed is the ground for your sake; in toil you shall eat
of it all the days of your life. Both thorns and thistles
it shall bring forth for you, and you shall eat the herb
of the field. In the sweat of your face you shall eat bread
till you return to the ground, for out of it you were taken;
for dust you are, and to dust you shall return."
Genesis 3:17-19, NKJV

... Just as through one man sin entered the world,
and death through sin, and thus death spread
to all men, because all sinned...
Romans 5:12, NKJV

The world as we know it today is ***not*** the world as God intended it. Nor
is the person in the mirror the man or woman the Creator originally

had in mind. The divine image in man has been obscured by sin and death. The garden has been transformed into a vale of tears. For the moment, *everything* is "situation abnormal." And the resulting obstacles to fulfillment, happiness, and holiness are more formidable than we sometimes realize.

Do I understand what it means to be fallen and flawed? Do I feel the utter desperation of the human condition? *question*

response

prayer

Show me, Father, what it means to be a cracked earthen pot (2 Corinthians 4:7). Help me to see myself as a vessel of clay, marred and spoiled but wholly yielded to the Potter's hand (Jeremiah 18:4). I thank You that You have seen my plight and initiated a plan for my restoration. Remind me that, though broken and blemished, I am even now a child of the King and that it has not yet been revealed what I shall become when I see Your face at last (1 John 3:2).

CONSEQUENCES

And the Lᴏʀᴅ God commanded the man, saying,
"Of every tree of the garden you may freely eat;
but of the tree of the knowledge of good and evil you
shall not eat, for in the day that you eat of it
you shall surely die."
Genesis 2:16, 17, NKJV

So all the days that Adam lived were
nine hundred and thirty years; and he died.
Genesis 5:5, NKJV

And you were dead in your trespasses and sins...
Ephesians 2:1, NASB

Death is primarily a spiritual reality. Adam did not drop to the ground the instant he tasted the forbidden fruit; it took more than nine centuries for the physical consequences of his disobedience to catch up with him. Yet *something* expired inside him as soon as he made the decision to discredit God's word and turn away from his heavenly Father's love. That inward separation from God and self is the essence and definition of death. It's also an inescapable part of our heritage as Adam's sons and daughters.

Do I weigh the consequences of my actions, or do I behave as if sin will have no long-term effects?

Grant me long-range vision, my God. Help me to see that my tomorrows will be shaped by the choices I make today. You are the Alpha and the Omega, the Beginning and the End (Revelation 1:8), the God of yesterday, today, and forever (Hebrews 13:8). Let me live with a constant awareness of Your presence. I praise You that though the wages of sin is death, the gift of God is eternal life in Christ Jesus our Lord (Romans 6:23).

THE CONFLICT WITHIN

For we know that the law is spiritual, but I am carnal,
sold under sin. For what I am doing, I do not understand.
For what I will to do, that I do not practice; but what
I hate, that I do... Now if I do what I will not to do,
it is no longer I who do it, but sin that dwells in me.
Romans 7:14, 15, 20, NKJV

I say then: Walk in the Spirit, and you shall not
fulfill the lust of the flesh. For the flesh lusts against
the Spirit, and the Spirit against the flesh;
and these are contrary to one another, so that you
do not do the things that you wish.
Galatians 5:16, 17, NKJV

All things are full of labor; man cannot express it. The eye
is not satisfied with seeing, nor the ear filled with hearing.
Ecclesiastes 1:8, NKJV

"Self-actualizers" face a thorny dilemma: because of the Fall, the self is at
war with itself. How does one follow one's inner desires when they cancel
each other out? Goodness eludes the virtuous. Illicit pleasures turn to
ashes in the sinner's mouth. What we think we want we seldom achieve,

reflection

and when we do achive it, we are rarely satisfied. No one consistently lives up to his or her own standard of goodness, whatever it may be. How can we fulfill our needs when we don't know what they are?

Have I hit the brick wall of my own inability to achieve self-integration? Or do I still believe that I can "put it all together" on my own?

question

response

prayer

I thank You, God, for those moments when You allow me to come to the end of myself, when my own efforts to do good or to be good are simply not enough. At such times I understand what Paul meant when he said, "When I am weak, then I am strong" (2 Corinthians 12:10), for it is in weakness that I am compelled to trust in Your sufficiency. I lean upon Your promise to perfect that which concerns me (Psalm 138:8). This is all my confidence and hope.

EMBRACING DISTRUST

... Cursed is the man who trusts in man and makes flesh his strength, whose heart departs from the LORD ...
Jeremiah 17:5, NKJV

The heart is deceitful above all things, and desperately wicked; who can know it? I, the LORD, search the heart, I test the mind, even to give to every man according to his ways, according to the fruit of his doings.
Jeremiah 17:9, 10, NKJV

For I know of nothing against myself, yet I am not justified by this; but He who judges me is the Lord.
1 Corinthians 4:4, NKJV

"Know yourself," said the sages of ancient Greece, for in knowing yourself you will know all things and find the path to personal fulfillment. The aphorism is as popular today as it was three thousand years ago. But is it realistic? In contrast to Greek philosophy, the Bible recommends skepticism with respect to the inward motions of the heart. That's because the human self, distorted and gone awry, can be self-deceiving. The wise man leans not on self-understanding but on the Lord, who sees all things.

In a pinch, do I trust in God's grace or rely on my own inclinations?

O Lord, I know the way of man is not in himself (Jeremiah 10:23). Deliver me from the deceitfulness of my own heart. Help me to see that my dreams and aspirations cannot be trusted unless and until they are made subject to Your sovereign will. If necessary, cause my plans and purposes to fail, that I may be driven to rely entirely upon Your unseen guidance. Remind me that while there is a way that seems right to a man, its end is the way of death (Proverbs 16:25).

DECLARATION OF DEPENDENCE

Now a certain ruler asked Him, saying,
"Good Teacher, what shall I do to inherit eternal life?"
So Jesus said to him, "Why do you call Me good?
No one is good but One, that is, God."
Luke 18:18, 19, NKJV

Truly God is good to Israel, to such as are pure
in heart. But as for me, my feet had almost
stumbled; my steps had nearly slipped.
Psalm 73:1, 2, NKJV

Trust in the LORD with all your heart, and lean
not on your own understanding.
Proverbs 3:5, NKJV

Even Christ, the incarnate Son, was constrained to say, "None is good but God." It was precisely as the **perfect man** that He was able to make this memorable declaration. At its heart, it's a **declaration of dependence** upon the heavenly Father. Jesus knew that the ultimate reference point for goodness, wisdom, and truth **cannot** lie within the human self. Men and women can never be complete until they learn to derive all their significance and worth from the One who created them.

Do I live by the guiding star of God's nature and character, or is my confidence centered in myself?

You, Lord, are the definition of all that is good and just. You are gracious and long-suffering, abounding in goodness and truth (Exodus 34:6). It is Your kindness that leads us to repentance (Romans 2:4). Without You, we cannot tell right from wrong, up from down, virtue from evil, life from death. Help me to rest in You as a weaned child leans against its mother (Psalm 131:2). My hope is in You alone from this time forth and forever.

GOD ONLY

... For I am God, and there is no other;
I am God, and there is none like Me.
Isaiah 46:9, NKJV

Hear, O Israel: The LORD our God, the LORD is one!
You shall love the LORD your God with all your heart,
with all your soul, and with all your strength.
Deuteronomy 6:4, 5, NKJV

No one has seen God at any time.
The only begotten Son, who is in the bosom
of the Father, He has declared Him.
John 1:18, NKJV

God *is*. This is the single most important fact in all the universe. The key to genuine living lies in the realization that everything centers around *Him*. To seek Him, know Him, glorify Him, and enjoy Him forever – this is the sum and substance of our intended destiny as human beings. That destiny remains open to us even in our flawed and sinful state, not as a result of

ANTHROPOLOGY: who is **Man**?

anything *we* have done, but purely because *He* has taken the initiative to search us out and draw us to Himself in the person of Jesus Christ.

Is my perspective God-centered or self-centered?

You alone are worthy, O Lord, to receive glory and honor and power, for You created all things and by Your will they exist and were created (Revelation 4:11). Let this be my creed, my song, and the consistent theme of my life. Make me a testimony to the all-embracing reality of Your eternal presence and indefatigable love. Without You, I can do nothing (John 15:5), but at Your right hand I inherit joys and pleasures forevermore (Psalm 16:11).

Now this is eternal life: that they may know you,

the only true God, and Jesus Christ, whom you have sent.

John 17:3 (NIV)

tour 4

Theology

who is **God**?

KNOWLEDGE AND RELATIONSHIP

For I desire mercy and not sacrifice, and the knowledge of God more than burnt offerings.
Hosea 6:6, NKJV

Now a certain ruler asked Him, saying, "Good Teacher, what shall I do to inherit eternal life?"
Luke 18:18, NKJV

And this is eternal life, that they may know You, the only true God, and Jesus Christ whom You have sent.
John 17:3, NKJV

God is the source and center of all things, the One in whom "we live and move and have our being" (Acts 17:28). It follows that *knowing God* – knowing Him, not as an object or a fact, but as a person within the context of an intimate *personal relationship* – is the ultimate goal of our existence. This, as Jesus said, is what it means to have eternal life: not merely *everlasting* life, but a *living connection* with the eternal Creator.

Do I understand the privilege God extends to me by inviting me into a personal relationship with Himself?

God of the universe, I realize that my small and feeble mind cannot begin to grasp the fullness of who You are. But I do know that You have called me to Yourself. Even this knowledge is too wonderful for me; it is high, I cannot attain it (Psalm 139:6). I can respond only by saying yes to Your invitation. Make me Your child. My goal is to know even as I am known (1 Corinthians 13:12) and to return Your love with all my heart, soul, mind, and strength (Matthew 22:37).

KNOWLEDGE ECLIPSED

For the earth will be filled with the knowledge of the
glory of the Lord, as the waters cover the sea.
Habakkuk 2:14, NKJV

For the wrath of God is revealed from heaven
against all ungodliness and unrighteousness of men,
who suppress the truth in unrighteousness,
because what may be known of God is manifest
in them, for God has shown it to them.
Romans 1:18, 19, NKJV

But even if our gospel is veiled, it is veiled
to those who are perishing, whose minds
the god of this age has blinded ...
2 Corinthians 4:3, 4, NKJV

reflection

Who is God? What is He like? Complete answers to these questions lie
beyond the range of our comprehension. And yet the Bible tells us that
we already know enough of God's character, having seen it reflected in
creation and in our own human nature, to be rendered fully accountable

for our choices and actions. Fearing the implications, we hide from the Truth and cast up shadows against the light. It's a characteristic mark of the age in which we live.

Am I aware of the subtle ways in which I deny what I already know about God?

Deliver me, Lord, again and again from the bondage of self-deception and self-imposed ignorance. Open my eyes to the miracle of Your love. Even Your visible, physical creation is filled with clear reminders of Your unseen power and divine nature. Whether I perceive it or not, I am swimming in a sea of Your goodness and grace. Take away the blinders of unbelief and give me the courage to face reality head-on. I know that I am without excuse if I shrink from this bracing challenge (Romans 1:20; Hebrews 10:38).

KNOWLEDGE DESIRED

As the deer pants for the water brooks,
so pants my soul for You, O God. My soul
thirsts for God, for the living God.
When shall I come and appear before God?
Psalm 42:1, 2, NKJV

For I know the thoughts that I think toward you,
says the LORD, thoughts of peace and not of evil,
to give you a future and a hope. Then you will call
upon Me and go and pray to Me, and I will listen
to you. And you will seek Me and find Me,
when you search for Me with all your heart.
Jeremiah 29:11-13, NKJV

Yet indeed I also count all things loss for the
excellence of the knowledge of Christ Jesus my Lord,
for whom I have suffered the loss of all things, and
count them as rubbish, that I may gain Christ ... that
I may know Him and the power of His resurrection,
and the fellowship of His sufferings, being
conformed to His death ...
Philippians 3:8, 10, NKJV

God. How is it possible that this name, this verbal symbol of power and mystery and perfection, has been reduced among us to the level of a mere expletive? Why are we not moved to tears, awe, and exultation at the very sound of it? To know God we must *want* Him more than we want anything else. And we will not want Him with that kind of earnestness until our sense of wonder is renewed – until we've caught a glimpse of the goodness, the beauty, the holiness, and the truth that He is.

Has religion inoculated me against the reality of God? Or do I ache to know and experience Him in the depths of my being?

Before I was afflicted, I went astray, but now I keep Your Word (Psalm 119:67). Afflict me more and more, dear Lord, with a burning thirst for Your presence. Light a fire of desire within me. Let me seek You diligently and without ceasing. With You, there is abundance of joy even in hardship and suffering. Without You, the greatest riches and pleasures are only dry leaves scattered on the wind.

KNOWLEDGE REVEALED

> Then God said, "Let there be light"; and there was light.
> **Genesis 1:3, NKJV**
>
> No one has seen God at any time. The only
> begotten Son, who is in the bosom of
> the Father, He has declared Him.
> **John 1:18, NKJV**
>
> All Scripture is given by inspiration of God, and
> is profitable for doctrine, for reproof, for correction, for
> instruction in righteousness, that the man of God may
> be complete, thoroughly equipped for every good work.
> **2 Timothy 3:16, 17, NKJV**

Sin deadens and obscures. So powerful are the distorting effects of disobedience and self-will that we fail to see the obvious. Our search for God becomes futile. It's like looking for light in a sealed box at the bottom of the sea. But God has not left us in this self-imposed gloom. He has spoken to us. His revealed Word, like a lightning bolt, shatters the walls of our prison. Next to creation itself, this is the greatest fact in the entire history of the universe.

Do I understand the significance of revelation? Do I cherish the gift God has given me in His written Word? *question*

response

prayer

I thank You, God, that You have not left me to find my own way in the darkness. I would never have known You if You had not spoken out of the silence and called me to Yourself. As it is, You have redeemed me and made me Your own through the power of Your Word, which cannot return to You void, but always accomplishes Your good pleasure (Isaiah 55:11). That Word is a lamp to my feet and a light to my path (Psalm 119:105). Help me to walk in that light every day of my life.

REVEALING KNOWLEDGE

So I said, "Woe is me, for I am undone!
Because I am a man of unclean lips, and I dwell
in the midst of a people of unclean lips; for my eyes
have seen the King, the LORD of Hosts."
Isaiah 6:5, NKJV

For the word of God is living and powerful,
and sharper than any two-edged sword, piercing
even to the division of soul and spirit, and of joints
and marrow, and is a discerner of the thoughts and
intents of the heart. And there is no creature hidden
from His sight, but all things are naked and open to
the eyes of Him to whom we must give account.
Hebrews 4:12, 13, NKJV

He who overcomes, I will make him a pillar in the
temple of My God, and he shall go out no more.
I will write on him the name of My God and the name
of the city of My God, the New Jerusalem,
which comes down out of heaven from My God.
And I will write on him My new name.
Revelation 3:12, NKJV

"Know yourself," advised the philosophers. But the Bible says, "Know **God** … and learn to see yourself in the light of **His** truth." The problem is that the picture of self that emerges in the process can be crushing. The more we subject ourselves to that light, the more we are driven to cry, "Woe is me!" But despair is not the final word; for to those who trust in His grace He grants a new name: a new identity and a **new self**, created for good works in Jesus Christ (Ephesians 2:10).

Am I willing to see myself as God sees me? Do I seek Him for His own sake and leave the consequences in His capable hands?

O Lord, my heart is open to You. You must increase and I must decrease (John 3:30). Do whatever it takes to accomplish Your will and perfect Your purposes in me. Through Your Word reveal Your Truth and show me who I really am in Your sight. Mold me into the new person You want me to become. By faith I acknowledge that I am a new creation in Christ, that old things have passed away and all things have been made new (2 Corinthians 5:17). Let me grow into a deeper realization and experience of this profound reality with every passing day.

KNOWLEDGE AND FACT

> The heavens declare the glory of God; and the
> firmament shows His handiwork. Day unto day utters
> speech, and night unto night reveals knowledge. There
> is no speech nor language where their voice is not
> heard. Their line has gone out through all the earth...
> **Psalm 19:1-4, NKJV**
>
> Come and see the works of God; He is awesome
> in His doing toward the sons of men.
> **Psalm 66:5, NKJV**
>
> For we can do nothing against the truth,
> but only for the truth.
> **2 Corinthians 13:8, NASB**

"We must not be afraid to follow the truth wherever it leads," declared Carl Sagan, celebrated science-popularizer of the 1980s.[2] Sagan may not have realized what he was saying. Scripture claims that scientific truth –that is, detailed **knowledge** (Latin *scientia*) of the objective facts and observable realities of the universe – leads inexorably to God. Understood rightly, the "stuff in the box" points to its Creator. Apparently Sagan didn't have the fortitude to draw the logical conclusions.

Do I fear the implications of the facts – of the universe understood on its own terms? If so, why?

question

response

prayer

Grant me courage to go forth into the world, armed with a deep knowledge of Your love and strengthened in the confidence that Truth, wherever it appears and whatever form it takes, is unconquerable. It is unconquerable because it flows from You alone and because it always leads back to its source. You are the Truth, Lord (John 14:6), and Your Word is Truth (John 17:17). Give me a tireless zeal for harmonizing the principles of Your Truth with the facts of life as I encounter them in this world. Help me to follow the Truth wherever it leads.

---

[2] Sagan, Carl (Producer). (1980). *Cosmos*. Los Angeles, CA: Cosmos Studios.

KNOWLEDGE AND WORSHIP

For you shall worship no other god, for the LORD,
whose name is Jealous, is a jealous God.
Exodus 34:14, NKJV

And the Word became flesh and dwelt among us,
and we beheld His glory, the glory as of the only
begotten of the Father, full of grace and truth ...
For the law was given through Moses, but grace
and truth came through Jesus Christ.
John 1:14, 17, NKJV

But "he who glories, let him glory in the LORD."
2 Corinthians 10:17, NKJV

Knowledge sought for its own sake becomes a dead and sterile thing. All knowledge – relational, factual, scientific – points to something beyond itself. It's a road that leads somewhere. The goal of the journey is God. Jesus Christ is the traveler's companion, mentor, and guide. Everything comes together at the point of *worship*: in the place where we can only bow before the *glory* of Him who is the center of all things, the definition of all Truth, and the only rightful object of our allegiance.

How do my various interests and pursuits lead me to a deeper place in my relationship with God?

O God, You have surrounded me with eloquent witnesses to the all-embracing fact of Your grace. The stars declare Your glory (Psalm 19:1). The mountains and hills sing before You. The trees of the field clap their hands at Your presence (Isaiah 55:12). My one desire is to join their chorus of praise. Help me to give You the glory due Your name. In all my studies, all my discoveries, all my labors, and all my delights, grant me the inspiration and impetus I need in order to reach the goal You have set before me. I want to worship You in the beauty of holiness (Psalm 29:2).

The heavens declare the glory of God;

the skies proclaim the work of his hands.

Day after day they pour forth speech;

night after night they display knowledge.

There is no speech or language

where their voice is not heard.

Their voice goes out into all the earth,

their words to the ends of the world.

Psalm 19:1-4 (NIV)

tour 5 *(part 1)*

Science

what is **True**?

UNIVERSAL SPEECH

The heavens declare the glory of God; and the firmament shows His handiwork ... There is no speech nor language where their voice is not heard.
Psalm 19:1, 3, NKJV

For since the creation of the world His invisible attributes are clearly seen, being understood by the things that are made, even His eternal power and Godhead, so that they are without excuse.
Romans 1:20, NKJV

So then faith comes by hearing, and hearing by the word of God. But I say, have they not heard? Yes indeed: "Their sound has gone out to all the earth, and their words to the ends of the world."
Romans 10:17, 18, NKJV

God has not left Himself without a witness. The universe is alive with voices that speak of His mercy and grace. His goodness and power peer out at us from behind the thinly glimmering veil of sea and sky. Stars and flowers alike proclaim His undying love. If the little children fall silent, the rocks themselves will cry out so that no one can enter a mitigating plea of ignorance. No one can say, "I am not responsible for what I have seen and heard," however little or much.

Am I alive or dead to the voice of God in the created world?

_____

_____

_____

_____

_____

_____

There is no place, O God, where I can go to flee from Your presence. In the uttermost parts of the sea, in the depths of hell, in the darkest reaches of interstellar space, You are there (Psalm 139:7-12). Nevertheless, without moving an inch, I can close my ears to what the cosmos tells me about Your invisible Truth. Draw me to Yourself and deliver me from the icy prison of my own self-imposed silence and ignorance.

THE HEART OF CREATION

"Where were you when I laid the foundations of
the earth? ... To what were its foundations fastened?
Or who laid its cornerstone, when the morning stars
sang together, and all the sons of God shouted for joy?"
Job 38:4, 6, 7, NKJV

Does not wisdom cry out, and understanding lift up
her voice? ... "When He prepared the heavens,
I was there ... Then I was beside Him as a master
craftsman; and I was daily His delight, rejoicing
always before Him, rejoicing in His inhabited world,
and my delight was with the sons of men."
Proverbs 8:1, 27, 30, 31, NKJV

For you shall go out with joy, and be led out
with peace; the mountains and the hills shall
break forth into singing before you, and all the trees
of the field shall clap their hands.
Isaiah 55:12, NKJV

Creation does not merely *speak* of its Creator – it shouts and dances and sings. At the heart of the universe is a living, intangible Something that animates and colors the whole from the inside out with music, poetry, vitality, and joy. The motion of the butterfly's wing, like the life of the butterfly itself, defies objective analysis. It eludes the intrusive probing of microscope and scalpel. To seek to capture it is like trying to weigh and measure the human soul.

Am I sensitive to the miracle of life, wonder, and joy that beats at the heart of the universe?

You, Lord, have done all things well. You have made the world and declared it **good** (Genesis 1:31), and good it remains despite the marring inroads of disobedience and sin. It sings Your song in the starlight and the sunset. From the tops of the mountains to the ocean deeps, it vibrates with Your pleasure and delight. Give me eyes to see and ears to hear the wonders that breathe all around me.

SOMETHING OR NOTHING?

In the beginning God created the heavens and
the earth. The earth was without form, and void; and
darkness was on the face of the deep. And the Spirit
of God was hovering over the face of the waters. Then
God said, "Let there be light"; and there was light.
Genesis 1:1-3, NKJV

Let all the earth fear the LORD; let all the inhabitants
of the world stand in awe of Him. For He spoke, and
it was done; He commanded, and it stood fast.
Psalm 33:8, 9, NKJV

By faith we understand that the worlds were framed
by the word of God, so that the things which are seen
were not made of things which are visible.
Hebrews 11:3, NKJV

The central problem of philosophy, according to Jean-Paul Sartre, is "Why
is there something rather than nothing?" Its corollary is equally baffling:
"How can something come from nothing?" The Bible resolves the issue by

setting the *nothing* and the *something* aside and focusing our attention on *Someone*. Creation, says Genesis, sprang into being *ex nihilo* – "out of nothing" – when *God spoke the word*. The source of the universe, then, is neither matter nor energy; it's *personality* and *personal communication*.

Have I pondered the deeper implications of the scriptural teaching that God spoke the worlds into existence?

Before the chaos, before the darkness, before the silence of the great deep, **You** were there, O God; for of You, **through** You, and **to** You are all things (Romans 11:36), and all things express the inner beauty of Your being. Ultimately, there is no greater, more profound, or more revealing statement that can be made about the universe than the one You have uttered Yourself: "I AM" (Exodus 3:14). Help me to explore the marvels of the world with this all-encompassing axiom in mind.

TIME AND ETERNITY

For a thousand years in Your sight are like yesterday
when it is past, and like a watch in the night.
Psalm 90:4, NKJV

Behold, the nations are as a drop in a bucket,
and are counted as the small dust on the scales;
look, He lifts up the isles as a very little thing.
Isaiah 40:15, NKJV

Beloved, do not forget this one thing, that
with the Lord one day is as a thousand years,
and a thousand years as one day.
2 Peter 3:8, NKJV

Any serious view of reality has to take account of eternity. Boundaries are
always arbitrary and artificial. Time, from this perspective – the *entirety*
of time, from beginning to end – is a mathematical point in the midst of
a shoreless sea. Expand it or multiply it as much as you please; relatively
speaking, it remains a dimensionless dot. It is too small to explain the

unexplainable. It cannot be stretched wide enough to eclipse mystery. It does nothing to eliminate the miraculous from the story of creation.

Do I live my life in the light of God's infinity and eternity? Or am I unduly impressed with human concepts of greatness?

This is my confession of faith: Jesus Christ, the same yesterday, today, and forever (Hebrews 13:8). Time may change some things, O Lord, but it cannot change You, neither can it erode the wonder of creation or minimize the miracle of life. Straw cannot become gold, and molecules cannot become thinking, reasoning souls – not in a thousand trillion years. If they can, we can only respond only by bowing down in worship. Help me to worship You from a sincere and childlike heart.

THE WEIGHT OF GLORY

The heavens declare the glory of God ...
Psalm 19:1, NKJV

..."Surely the LORD our God has shown us His glory
and His greatness, and we have heard His voice
from the midst of the fire. We have seen this day
that God speaks with man; yet he still lives."
Deuteronomy 5:24, NKJV

But You, O LORD, are a shield for me, my glory
and the One who lifts up my head.
Psalm 3:3, NKJV

And the Word became flesh and dwelt among
us, and we beheld His glory, the glory as of the only
begotten of the Father, full of grace and truth.
John 1:14, NKJV

The heart of the universe beats with something more than mere energy, wonder, and delight. Pulsing at the center of everything else, like the nucleus of an atom, is a shining core of *glory*. *Glory* is the sensible manifestation of the inward essence of a *Person*. God's personality seeps through the cracks and pores of everything He has made. It presses upon us in the miraculous revelation of His Word, the embodiment of His wisdom. It confronts us in the face of Jesus Christ.

Have I experienced the immensity of God's presence in nature, in His Word, and in the person of Christ?

How is it, Father, that I am not crushed beneath the weight of Your personal presence and power? You call to me in the mountain snows and the flowers of the field. You declare Your will, Your wisdom, and Your love in words of human speech. You visit Your people in Jesus Christ and put Your Spirit within their physical bodies (1 Corinthians 6:19). Why do we not, like Isaiah, cry for mercy at every moment (Isaiah 6:5)? Why do we fail to tremble with fear and joy? Grant me a heart to marvel and exult in these gracious manifestations of Your glory.

THE GREAT QUESTION

"Who is this who darkens counsel by words
without knowledge? Now prepare yourself like a man;
I will question you, and you shall answer Me."
Job 38:2, 3, NKJV

What profit has a man from all his labor in which he toils
under the sun? One generation passes away, and another
generation comes; but the earth abides forever ... All
things are full of labor; man cannot express it. The eye is
not satisfied with seeing, nor the ear filled with hearing.
Ecclesiastes 1:3, 4, 8, NKJV

If in this life only we have hope in Christ,
we are of all men the most pitiable.
1 Corinthians 15:19, NKJV

Among the more "useful" Christmas presents that poet Dylan Thomas
received as a child were "books that told me everything about the wasp,
except why."[3] Young Thomas's books were quintessentially scientific.
Science can analyze, assess, describe, dissect, and reconstruct. As a key

to knowledge and power, its potency is practically unlimited. And yet it cannot answer the most pressing question of all: *why*? Meaning and significance are altogether beyond the range of its vision.

Do I understand the natural limitations of human knowledge and scientific investigation?

Father in heaven, I confess that the purposes, plans, goals, and counsels that You have built into creation are unsearchable, unknowable, and past all finding out unless You choose to reveal them (Romans 11:33; Colossians 1:26). Make me mindful of the mystery that dwells at the heart of all things, a mystery that finds resolution only as it dawns upon us in the face of Christ. Preserve me from the vanity – and despair – of seeking ultimate truth in circumstantial details.

---

[3] Dylan Thomas, *A Child's Christmas in Wales* (Boston: David R. Godine, 1984), 20-21.

BUILT-IN CLUES

Can you bind the cluster of the Pleiades, or loose
the belt of Orion? Can you bring out Mazzaroth in its
season? Or can you guide the Great Bear with its cubs?
Do you know the ordinances of the heavens?
Job 38:31-33, NKJV

Thus says the LORD, who gives the sun for a light by day,
the ordinances of the moon and the stars for a light by
night, who disturbs the sea, and its waves roar (the LORD
of Hosts is His name): "If those ordinances depart from
before Me, says the LORD, then the seed of Israel shall
also cease from being a nation before Me forever."
Jeremiah 31:35, 36, NKJV

For since the creation of the world His
invisible attributes are clearly seen, being
understood by the things that are made, even
His eternal power and Godhead ...
Romans 1:20, NKJV

One of several terms the psalmists use to describe the written Word of
God is a Hebrew noun we render as "statute" or "ordinance" (see Psalm

119:16). An "ordinance" is *fixed* and **unchangeable**. As a result, it's also predictable and reliable. Significantly, Jeremiah and the author of Job perceive similar "ordinances" in the workings of nature. It is this built-in order and stability, which Paul regards as evidence of the Creator's hand, that makes scientific investigation of the universe possible.

Do I appreciate the extent to which the scientific method is dependent upon biblical assumptions and a Christian worldview?

Among the good and perfect gifts that come down from You, O Father of lights, is **knowledge** of every kind: spiritual, historical, sociological, physical, and biological. Like clockwork, the sun rises and sets according to Your unchanging design (Ecclesiastes 1:5). The deer and the wild mountain goats bear their young in conformity with Your plan (Job 39:1-4). By Your wisdom, patterns emerge out of chaos. Exploration, experimentation, and meaningful interaction with nature become viable possibilities for rational human beings. I confess this to You in all humility, and I thank You for the incomprehensible marvel of Your grace.

For since the creation of the world God's invisible

qualities—his eternal power and divine nature—

have been clearly seen, being understood from

what has been made, so that men are without excuse. ...

Although they claimed to be wise, they became

fools and exchanged the glory of the

immortal God for images made to look

like mortal man and birds and

animals and reptiles.

Romans 1:20, 22-23 (NIV)

tour **5** *(part 2)*

Science

what is **True**?

"THE CHIEF AIM"

The words of the wise are like goads, and the words of
scholars are like well-driven nails, given by one Shepherd.
Ecclesiastes 12:11, NKJV

Jesus said to him, "You shall love the LORD your God
with all your heart, with all your soul, and with all
your mind. This is the first and great commandment.
Matthew 22:37, 38, NKJV

Though I have the gift of prophecy, and understand
all mysteries and all knowledge, and though
I have all faith, so that I could remove mountains,
but have not love, I am nothing.
1 Corinthians 13:2, NKJV

The chief aim of science, according to astronomer Johannes Kepler,
is to elucidate the "God-imposed order and harmony" of nature. The
chief end of man, according to *The Westminster Catechism*, is "to
glorify God, and to enjoy Him forever."[4] Faith and science, then, are
supposed to work together. As our understanding of the world expands,

so should our love for its Maker. The particulars – from stars to cells to shellfish – inspire wonder, and wonder directs the heart to the universal Shepherd of souls.

Have I pondered the ways in which "secular" and scientific knowledge can actually enhance my love for God?

All praise, honor, and glory belong to You, O Lord. Here in these last days You have spoken to us through Your Son, just as You created the worlds through Him at the beginning of time (Hebrews 1:1-3). Without Him was nothing made that has been made (John 1:3), and everything speaks of His grace, for He is the One in whom all things consist (Colossians 1:17). Let this thought be the creed and capstone of my life.

---

[4] *The Westminster Shorter Catechism*, Q1, A1; in *The Book of Confessions of the United Presbyterian Church in the U.S.A.* (New York: General Assembly of the UPCUSA, 1970).

THE FOREST AND THE TREES

...It is written, "Man shall not live by bread alone,
but by every word that proceeds from the mouth of God."
Matthew 4:4, NKJV; cf. Deuteronomy 8:3

...Hearing you will hear and shall not understand,
and seeing you will see and not perceive; for the
hearts of this people have grown dull, their ears are
hard of hearing and their eyes they have closed,
lest they should see with their eyes and hear with their
ears, lest they should understand with their hearts
and turn, so that I should heal them.
Matthew 13:14, 15, NKJV; cf. Isaiah 6:9, 10

...Although they knew God, they did not glorify Him
as God, nor were thankful, but became futile in their
thoughts, and their foolish hearts were darkened.
Romans 1:21, NKJV

reflection

Is seeing believing? Is experience knowledge? Apparently not. The
Israelites saw the miracle of the manna in the desert. They knew what it

was like to have their bodily needs supplied. But they didn't perceive the unseen reality behind these physical facts. Like researchers who analyze the mechanics of creation but never notice the Creator, they couldn't see the forest for the trees. Deprived of the gift of divine vision, they failed to make the connection between details and overall design.

Do I look for the hidden pattern that gives unity and meaning to the pieces of life's puzzle?

Deliver me, my God, from the blindness that sees without seeing. Take away the scales from my eyes (Acts 9:18), that the light of Your Truth, revealed in earth, sea, sky, and my own human nature, may strike in upon me with the fullness of its illuminating force. Show me the futility of attempting to build a worldview out of the broken bricks of my own observations and experience. You alone hold the key to the riddle of life.

BLIND RESISTANCE

The fool has said in his heart, "There is no God."
They are corrupt, they have done abominable works,
there is none who does good.
Psalm 14:1, NKJV

Professing to be wise, they became fools,
and changed the glory of the incorruptible God
into an image made like corruptible man ...
Romans 1:22, 23, NKJV

For we do not wrestle against flesh and blood,
but against principalities, against powers, against
the rulers of the darkness of this age, against spiritual
hosts of wickedness in the heavenly places.
Ephesians 6:12, NKJV

The Watchmaker, says Richard Dawkins, is blind: biology is the study
of complicated things that merely "*give the appearance* of having been
designed for a purpose." But how can one disregard appearance and still
make use of the scientific method? What leads an intelligent man like

Dawkins to make such an absurd and foolish statement? What, indeed, but intense spiritual conflict. Blaise Pascal was right: men discredit the Christian faith because "they hate it and are afraid it may be true."

question

Am I aware of the spiritual dimensions of the conflict between faith and science?

response

prayer

You have taught me, Father, that no part of human life is free from the effects of the Cosmic Battle. Love is seldom pure, motives are usually mixed, and the quest for knowledge is rarely objective and altruistic. We see what we want to see, and our investigations yield the results we want them to yield. Guard my heart against this kind of self-deception. When foes of the faith come against me armed with scientific facts, give me eyes to discern the true condition of their hearts. Remind me that the weapons of this warfare are not carnal, but mighty in You for pulling down strongholds (2 Corinthians 10:4).

AMAZING GRACE

I will wait on the LORD, who hides His face from
the house of Jacob; and I will hope in Him.
Isaiah 8:17, NKJV

And Elisha prayed, and said, "LORD, I pray, open
his eyes that he may see." Then the LORD opened
the eyes of the young man, and he saw.
2 Kings 6:17 NKJV

... Christ, in whom are hidden all
the treasures of wisdom and knowledge.
Colossians 2:2, 3, NKJV

"I once was lost, but now am found," wrote the Reverend John Newton;
"was blind, but now I see."[5] Not only does fallen man *refuse* to recognize
the obvious; there is an important sense in which he *cannot* recognize it.
God, in His holiness, *hides* Himself from those whose hearts are tainted
with bitterness and sin. The ability to see His truth is a gift of sheer
mercy and grace. We must always bear this in mind when dealing with

rationalistic unbelief. There is more to this struggle than meets the eye. Am I sufficiently grateful for the gift of God's enlightening grace? Do I pray that others may receive this gift as well?

God, I thank You for opening my eyes (John 9:25). Apart from Your grace, which draws the veil aside and grants me access to the indescribable treasures concealed within the humility, meekness, and weakness of Jesus Christ, I would be lost and cut off from Your goodness and glory. Make me a vessel of Your mercy. Use me to impart this same grace to others. Fill me with Your love and help me to be patient with those who seem stubbornly unwilling to acknowledge the great truths You have revealed about Yourself in creation.

---

[5] John Newton, "Amazing Grace", from the collection *Olney Hymns,* by John Newton and William Cowper; first published 1779

day 5

IDEAS OF CONSEQUENCE

"The lamp of the body is the eye. If therefore
your eye is good, your whole body will be full of light.
But if your eye is bad, your whole body will be full
of darkness. If therefore the light that is in you is
darkness, how great is that darkness!"
Matthew 6:22, 23, NKJV

And He said, "What comes out of a man, that defiles
a man. For from within, out of the heart of men,
proceed evil thoughts, adulteries, fornications, murders,
thefts, covetousness, wickedness, deceit, lewdness,
an evil eye, blasphemy, pride, foolishness. All these
evil things come from within and defile a man."
Mark 7:20-23, NKJV

"Either make the tree good and its fruit good,
or else make the tree bad and its fruit bad;
for a tree is known by its fruit."
Matthew 12:33, NKJV

Ideas have consequences. Worldview makes all the difference in the world.

People ***behave*** according to their perception of reality. If "survival of the fittest" is the name of the game, then fitness and survival are paramount. But if the Cross is the most important fact in human history, self-sacrifice and the interests of others become the dominant considerations. It's no wonder that Adolf Hitler appealed to Darwinian theory in justification of his National Socialist vision.

question

Do I realize how my understanding of the universe impacts my actions? Conversely, do I live as if what I say I believe is *really* real?

response

prayer

Purify my eye, O Lord. Fill me, body, soul, and spirit, with the light of Your life-giving Truth. Grant me a vision of life and reality drawn solely from the clear, life-giving stream of Your Word, so that, rooted and grounded in faith (Colossians 2:7), I may grow up into Christ, a healthy, well-watered tree bringing forth fruit in due season (Psalm 1:3), glorifying You with good works and wholesome deeds (Matthew 5:16).

UNIVERSAL CONTEXT

Now the LORD had said to Abram: "Get out
of your country, from your family, and from your
father's house, to a land that I will show you.
I will make you a great nation; I will bless you and
make your name great; and you shall be a blessing."
Genesis 12:1, 2, NKJV

Therefore know that only those who are of faith
are sons of Abraham. And the Scripture, foreseeing
that God would justify the Gentiles by faith,
preached the gospel to Abraham beforehand, saying,
"In you all the nations shall be blessed."
Galatians 3:7, 8, NKJV

As in the realm of natural history, so where the story of humanity is
concerned, **particulars** have no meaning apart from the pattern of the
universal plan. Divorced from the miracle of life, a carbon molecule
is nothing but an isolated particle of matter. Similarly, Abram's journey
from Ur to Canaan, momentous as it must have seemed at the time,
assumes full significance only within the story of Christ and His church.
God Himself is the glue that binds the pieces of the puzzle together.

Is my sense of identity dependent upon my grasp of God's larger plan? Or do I see everything in terms of my own personal agenda?

question

response

prayer

Father in heaven, I thank You for giving me a role to play in the unfolding of Your overarching plan. Help me to see myself as You see me: not as an insignificant drop in the ocean of matter and energy, nor as a meaningless cog on an endlessly turning wheel, but as a small though important actor in the drama of which You are both author and director. You work all things together according to the counsel of Your will, not only for the good of those who love You (Romans 8:28), but also for the praise of Your glory (Ephesians 1:14).

ETERNITY AND TIME

And the Lord said, "I have surely seen the oppression
of My people who are in Egypt, and have heard
their cry because of their taskmasters, for I know
their sorrows. So I have come down to deliver them
out of the hand of the Egyptians ..."
Exodus 3:7, 8, NKJV

"Are not five sparrows sold for two copper coins?
And not one of them is forgotten before God. But the
very hairs of your head are all numbered. Do not fear
therefore; you are of more value than many sparrows."
Luke 12:6, 7, NKJV

But concerning the times and the seasons, brethren,
you have no need that I should write to you ...
1 Thessalonians 5:1, NKJV

Both "times" – the span of the ages (Greek *chronoi*) – *and* "seasons" –
the opportune moments of our lives (Greek *karoi*) – are important to
God. Both have a place within the purview of His overall purpose and

plan. Though He stands outside of time, as the Everlasting Father, He condescends to step into its stream as a concession to love. He hears our cries, feels our sorrows, and knows our concerns, and so He weaves the threads of our lives into the plot of His grand, ongoing story.

question

Do I realize that God is with me every moment of the day, directing the details of my life in accord with His all-encompassing will?

response

prayer

I thank You, Lord, that You are not limited by time. You live in the eternal present. You see the years and moments of my existence at a single glance. From birth to death and beyond, I live under the guidance of Your watchful eye. How precious are Your thoughts to me! How great is the sum of them! If I should count them, they would be more in number than the sand; when I awake, I am still with You (Psalm 139:17, 18). Let this awareness never depart from me as I pass through this world and enact the scenes You have assigned to me in Your drama.

Remember the former things, those of long ago;

I am God, and there is no other;

I am God, and there is none like me.

I make known the end from the beginning,

from ancient times, what is still to come.

I say: My purpose will stand,

and I will do all that I please.

From the east I summon a bird of prey;

from a far-off land, a man to fulfill my purpose.

What I have said, that will I bring about;

what I have planned, that will I do.

Isaiah 46:9-11 (NIV)

tour **6**

History

whose **Story**?

THE ARTFUL DIRECTOR

The counsel of the LORD stands forever,
the plans of His heart to all generations.
Psalm 33:11, NKJV

Now a certain man drew a bow at random, and struck
the king of Israel between the joints of his armor ...
1 Kings 22:34, NKJV

In Him also we have obtained an inheritance, being
predestined according to the purpose of Him who
works all things according to the counsel of His will.
Ephesians 1:11, NKJV

Author H. G. Wells once described God as the "frantic director" of a
play gone hopelessly out of control. Wells failed to appreciate the subtlety
of an artist who *uses* apparent flaws and blunders to accomplish His design.
God was in charge when King Ahab fell before a "random" arrow. He
"ordains whatsoever comes to pass,"[6] not only *in spite of* chance, sin, and
man's free will, but *by means of* them. This is the mystery that lies at the
heart of history – the key to the story that contains and explains all others.

Is my life frantic and chaotic? Or does it reflect an ordered confidence in the grace and goodness of a loving and sovereign God?

question

response

prayer

Lord, my hope is stayed on You. You are my Keeper and the Shade upon my right hand. Without Your permission, the sun cannot strike me by day nor the moon by night. You neither slumber nor sleep, great Defender, Protector, and Guide (Psalm 121:3-6). I confess that my times are in Your hands; You have appointed my limits that I cannot pass (Job 14:5). Accept my praise and bless me, I pray, O gracious Author of the tale of my days.

---

[6] *Westminster Confession of Faith*, Chapter III, Section 1.

NAMES AND STORIES

So Adam gave names to all cattle, to the birds
of the air, and to every beast of the field.
Genesis 2:20, NKJV

"Fear not, for I have redeemed you; I have called
you by your name; you are Mine."
Isaiah 43:1, NKJV

"So the LORD brought us out of Egypt with
a mighty hand and with an outstretched arm,
with great terror and with signs and wonders.
He has brought us to this place and has given us
this land, 'a land flowing with milk and honey.'"
Deuteronomy 26:8, 9, NKJV

The beginning of the gospel
of Jesus Christ, the Son of God ...
Mark 1:1, NKJV

Throughout the Bible we encounter the idea that *significance* and *reality* are closely linked with verbal symbols. A person or thing becomes its true self by receiving its true *name*. Likewise, a people discovers its identity by embracing its *story* – a kind of "name" in extended narrative form. Israel was defined by the Exodus. The church lives by the gospel – "the good story" (Old English *godspell*) – of Jesus Christ. Without our story, we cannot understand how we fit into God's larger plan for the cosmos.

Do I know the story that defines me as a person and a member of Christ's body? Do I allow it to shape the particulars of my everyday life?

I thank You, God, for giving me a name, a story, and a place in Your master plan. In Christ, You have told me who I am. Through His life, death, and resurrection, You have convinced me that I am significant **and** loved. I understand that **He** is the sum of all things, the firstborn of creation, the head of the church (Colossians 1:15, 18). Help me to live in the light and power of **His** story – the glorious and everlasting gospel. Let His Word dwell in me richly (Colossians 3:16), that it might become a lamp to my feet and a light to my path (Psalm 119:105).

THE BIGGER PICTURE

"But as for you, you meant evil against me;
but God meant it for good, in order to bring it about
as it is this day, to save many people alive."
Genesis 50:20, NKJV

Blessed be the God and Father of our Lord Jesus Christ,
the Father of mercies and God of all comfort, who
comforts us in all our tribulation, that we may be able
to comfort those who are in any trouble, with the
comfort with which we ourselves are comforted by God.
2 Corinthians 1:3, 4, NKJV

Joseph: outcast, slave, and aide to the world's most powerful ruler.
Paul: Pharisee, persecutor, and preacher of a faith he once despised. Two
distinct stories, two different places and times. But the protagonists shared
a common perspective. Both knew that trials and triumphs are about
something more than personal sorrow and success. Under God, they saw
their own stories as episodes in a much larger narrative. As a result, their
lives impacted others to a degree beyond all reasonable expectation.

Do I have the ability to look beyond my own circumstances and trust in the greater purposes of God?

Jesus, I confess that You are the Lord, not only of my life and my situation, but of **every** life and **every** situation across the entire span of human history. One day every knee will bow and every tongue confess that You are the Master of all (Philippians 2:10, 11). Help me to make the same confession in the way I respond to my daily circumstances. Whether I rise or fall, laugh or cry, suffer or succeed, let me rejoice in the knowledge that, in the unfolding of **Your** story, these experiences may yet become a pathway of spiritual stepping stones for others.

SOVEREIGNTY DISPUTE

There are many plans in a man's heart,
nevertheless the LORD's counsel – that will stand.
Proverbs 19:21, NKJV

...That Day will not come unless the falling away comes
first, and the man of sin is revealed, the son of
perdition, who opposes and exalts himself above all
that is called God or that is worshiped, so that he
sits as God in the temple of God, showing
himself that he is God.
2 Thessalonians 2:3, 4, NKJV

Come now, you who say, "Today or tomorrow we
will go to such and such a city, spend a year there,
buy and sell, and make a profit"; whereas you do not
know what will happen tomorrow. For what is your life?
It is even a vapor that appears for a little time and
then vanishes away. Instead you ought to say,
"If the Lord wills, we shall live and do this or that."
James 4:13-15, NKJV

There are at least three methods of resisting the idea of God's sovereignty over the story of mankind. We can forget Him, as the children of Israel

HISTORY: whose **Story**?

did time and time again. We can revise the story to suit our own personal preferences. We can even deny it altogether, as postmodern thinkers do. But in every case the motive is the same. The underlying issue is control: *we* want to be in charge. This is how the field of historical inquiry becomes a battle front in the Cosmic Conflict between truth and lies.

question

Am I willing to submit to God's authority in every area of my life? Or do I look for ways to assert my own agenda?

response

prayer

I know, O Lord, that You alone are God. You have made us and we are entirely Yours (Psalm 100:3). Let this great Truth shape my perception of my own story—past, present, and future. Let it inform my reading of history and color my understanding of Your dealings with Your people. I acknowledge Your authority, goodness, and grace. I confess that Your mercy is everlasting, Your Truth enduring to all generations. May I never forget that, come what may, You have recorded my name in your heavenly Book of Life.

MEMORIAL STONES

Then he spoke to the children of Israel, saying,
"When your children ask their fathers in time
to come, saying, 'What are these stones?' then you
shall let your children know, saying, 'Israel crossed
over this Jordan on dry land.'"
Joshua 4:21, 22, NKJV

"Remember the former things of old, for I am God,
and there is no other; I am God, and there is none
like Me, declaring the end from the beginning, and from
ancient times things that are not yet done, saying,
'My counsel shall stand, and I will do all My pleasure.'"
Isaiah 46:9, 10, NKJV

And He took bread, gave thanks and broke it,
and gave it to them, saying, "This is My body which
is given for you; do this in remembrance of Me."
Luke 22:19, NKJV

There is one way to stand firm in the Cosmic Battle: we must remain
anchored to the Rock. Like the people who passed through Jordan, we

need memorial stones – tangible reminders of solid truths – to help us *remember* what God has done to bring us to this point in the journey. The past is the key to the present, and the present is the bridge to the future. And it is in *remembering* Christ's once-for-all sacrifice on the cross that we fit ourselves for citizenship in the coming kingdom of God.

What practical steps do I take to keep Christ, His kingdom, and my place in His ongoing story clearly before my mind's eye at all times?

O Lord, make my heart a sanctuary dedicated to the memory of Your mighty deeds, a shrine in which Your acts of intervention and redemption are commemorated in daily festivals of joy. Let Your Word be inscribed upon the tablets of my heart and written upon the doorposts of my mind (Deuteronomy 6:9; Jeremiah 31:33). Confirm me in my resolution to build and maintain this temple to Your faithfulness. Let me never forget the wondrous ways in which You have demonstrated Your unfailing love for me.

HUMAN HISTORY AND HUMAN ORDER

So God created man in His own image; in the image
of God He created him; male and female He created them.
Genesis 1:27, NKJV

For since the creation of the world His
invisible attributes are clearly seen, being understood
by the things that are made ...
Romans 1:20, NKJV

For God is not the author of confusion, but of peace,
as in all the churches of the saints.
1 Corinthians 14:33, NKJV

History is more than a collection of names and dates. It's an ***ordered account*** of the story of God and man. Man builds, arranges, organizes. In so doing, he can't help but mirror the nature of the One in whose image he is made. The tales he tells, the cultures he creates, the institutions he invents – ***all*** reflect the same regularity, fitness, and symmetry that shine down on us from the stars or look up at us out of the structure of the cell. Man's penchant for order betrays his unique heritage as the ***Imago Dei***.

Do I understand that human society bears the imprint of God's image in man, and thus represents a special case of divine revelation in nature?

Beauty, balance, order, proportion – You, Lord, are the summation and epitome of all these things. Your fingerprints are on the things You have made, particularly on the life of man, who is the appointed regent of Your creation. Reveal to me the wonders that lie hidden within this profound and fundamental truth. Show me how the structures implicit in human society reflect Your goodness and grace. We are Your workmanship (Ephesians 2:10), and You are our peace (Ephesians 2:14). Help me to approach my brothers and sisters with these principles in mind.

THE RELATIONAL CORE

Then God said, "Let Us make man in Our image,
according to Our likeness ..."
Genesis 1:26, NKJV

In the beginning was the Word, and the Word
was with God, and the Word was God.
John 1:1, NKJV

"Father, I desire that they also whom You gave Me
may be with Me where I am, that they may behold
My glory which You have given Me; for You loved Me
before the foundation of the world."
John 17:24 NKJV

Before the world began or anything was made that has been made, there
was *relationship*. It existed from all eternity within the triune Godhead
itself: three distinct persons loving and delighting in one another in a
single divine essence, the Son begotten of the Father, the Spirit proceeding
from the Father and the Son. This relational component is central to the
significance of the divine image in man. Like their Maker, human beings
are designed to function in a context of personal interaction.

Do I understand the meaning of my life in terms of God and other people? Or am I determined to "make it on my own"?

No one can exist as a solitary, disconnected island. You, God, are the first, foremost, and greatest example of the timeless Truth. Where there is no relationship, there is no life; that is why the Bible declares that You **are** love (1 John 4:8). I freely confess that, apart from Christ, my life is empty and meaningless. By the same token, I admit that I cannot be whole in isolation from other people. For how can I love Jesus, whom I have not seen, if I do not love my brother, whom I **have** seen (1 John 4:20)? Enable me to cherish and respect every person who crosses my path today.

"Therefore a man shall leave his father and mother and hold fast to his wife, and the two shall become one flesh." This mystery is profound, and I am saying that it refers to Christ and the church.

Ephesians 5:31-32 (ESV)

tour 7

Sociology
the divine **Imprint**

THE ONE AND THE MANY

Can two walk together, unless they are agreed?
Amos 3:3, NKJV

"For in Him we live and move and have
our being, as also some of your own poets have said,
'For we also are His offspring.'"
Acts 17:28, NKJV

...There is neither Greek nor Jew, circumcised
nor uncircumcised, barbarian, Scythian, slave nor free,
but Christ is all and in all."
Colossians 3:11, NKJV

The Christian doctrine of the Trinity resolves one of the greatest of all philosophical problems: the question of *The One and The Many*. Is the universe *one thing* or many *different things*? How can it hang together and yet display such variety? Similarly, how can you and I enter into true relationship with one another and still retain our separate identities? The answer, of course, is that *unity in diversity* is inherent to the very nature of God Himself. He has made us, and we bear the stamp of His image.

Do I recognize interpersonal relationship, community, and cooperation as the divine miracles they really are?

Lord, I stand amazed at Your wisdom and might. You hold all things together by the power of Your matchless love. As Father, Son, and Holy Spirit, You are distinctly Three, yet indivisibly One. I praise You for the beauty of this great mystery. I see it reflected and manifested in every aspect of the world You have created and the structures You have established for happy and harmonious human relations. Grant me the grace to live my life and order my interactions with others in such a way that I, too, may proclaim the glory of Your triune majesty.

"IT IS NOT GOOD ..."

And the Lord God said, "It is not good that man should be alone; I will make him a helper comparable to him."
Genesis 2:18, NKJV

Two are better than one, because they have a good reward for their labor. For if they fall, one will lift up his companion. But woe to him who is alone when he falls, for he has no one to help him up. Again, if two lie down together, they will keep warm; but how can one be warm alone? Though one may be overpowered by another, two can withstand him. And a threefold cord is not quickly broken.
Ecclesiastes 4:9-12, NKJV

Even in paradise, in a state of sinless innocence – even while walking in the garden with his Creator – Adam remained incomplete. The implication is clear: we cannot know God fully in isolation. Aloneness is inconsistent with His nature and thus nonconducive to a genuine experience of His character. It is in togetherness that we discover, not only who *we* are, but also who *He* is. Herein lies the key to the meaning of *everything* – and the seeds of the biblical doctrine of *incarnation*.

Have I come to the realization that my relationship with God can never be a purely private and personal affair?

Thank You, God, for revealing Yourself to me **in the flesh** (John 1:14, 18) – not only in Jesus Christ, but also through the gift of other people. You have ordained my birth into a natural family (Psalm 127:3), granted me a role in the larger human community (Jeremiah 29:7), and grafted me into the ongoing life of Your chosen people (Romans 11:24). I confess that I often take these blessings for granted. Sometimes I even complain about them and seek to be rid of them. Help me instead to know You better by seeing You in the face of my neighbor.

STRUCTURE AND PURPOSE

Thus says the LORD, who gives the sun
for a light by day, the ordinances of the moon
and the stars for a light by night ...
Jeremiah 31:35, NKJV

...[Let us] grow up in all things into Him, who is the
Head – Christ – from whom the whole body, joined
and knit together by what every joint supplies,
according to the effective working by which
every part does its share, causes growth of the
body for the edifying of itself in love.
Ephesians 4:15, 16, NKJV

Let all things be done decently and in order.
1 Corinthians 14:40, NKJV

It is not enough to say that the universe is all about relationships. **Ordered** relationships are the only kind that will do. The Father **begets** the Son; the Spirit **proceeds** from the Father **and** the Son. Each person of the Trinity fills a unique role within the Godhead, just as the earth orbits the sun and the moon revolves around the earth. It is the same in the realm of human interaction. Where there is structure, there is life, health, and peace; whereas death and disorder may rightly be regarded as synonymous terms.

Do I approach the relationships of my life – at home, at church, or in the workplace – with a deep appreciation of the importance of God-ordained structure and order?

Father, I know that all my connections and dealings with other people have a place within Your wise and perfect plan for my life. You have fashioned me as an intricate unity (Job 10:8). Accordingly, there is not a relationship within the circle of my experience that falls outside the purview of Your sovereign will. Whether as parent or child, husband or wife, employer, employee, adviser, servant, or friend, I have a divinely ordered purpose to fulfill. Make me mindful of that purpose and enable me to walk consistently in its light.

AUTHORITY AND SUBMISSION

Let every soul be subject to the governing authorities.
For there is no authority except from God, and
the authorities that exist are appointed by God.
Romans 13:1, NKJV

...Be subject to one another in the fear of Christ.
Wives, be subject to your own husbands, as to the
Lord. For the husband is the head of the wife, as Christ
also is the head of the church, He Himself being the
Savior of the body. But as the church is subject to
Christ, so also the wives ought to be to their husbands
in everything. Husbands, love your wives, just as Christ
also loved the church and gave Himself up for her ...
Ephesians 5:21-25, NASB

Children, obey your parents in the Lord, for this is right.
Ephesians 6:1, NKJV

Where there is structure, there must also be diversification and subordination. A body, to be whole, needs both head *and* feet. *Equality*, that most important of contemporary values, does not imply *sameness*. If the ship of state or family or business is to stay afloat, personal ambition will have to give way to corporate and communal considerations. Some must lead while others follow, some sacrifice while others serve. This is the divine rule of order for *every* natural system and *every* social sphere.

question

Do I abdicate authority? Refuse the subordinate role? Or do I see submission and authority as equally conducive to the common good?

response

prayer

Lord, grant me a deeper understanding and appreciation of my unique place in each of the spheres wherein You have called me to serve. Teach me to submit myself to others for Christ's sake. Let me find joy in doing for Jesus what I would commonly do for myself. May all my words and actions be dedicated to the advancement of Your glory (1 Corinthians 10:31). Help me to obey You from the heart, not with eye service, as a pleaser of men, but as a bond servant of Jesus Christ (Ephesians 6:5, 6).

BROKEN BONDS

...And Adam and his wife hid themselves from the
presence of the LORD God among the trees of
the garden. ... And [God] said, "Who told you that you
were naked? Have you eaten from the tree of which I
commanded you that you should not eat?"
Then the man said, "The woman whom You gave
to be with me, she gave me of the tree, and I ate."
Genesis 3:8, 11, 12, NKJV

...Take heed to your spirit, and let none deal
treacherously with the wife of his youth.
"For the LORD God of Israel says that He hates divorce,
for it covers one's garment with violence.
Malachi 2:15, 16, NKJV

For we ourselves were also once foolish, disobedient,
deceived, serving various lusts and pleasures, living
in malice and envy, hateful and hating one another.
Titus 3:3, NKJV

Sin is not simply a matter of breaking rules. It's essentially a question of breaking **bonds**. When we seek our own way, we cut ourselves off from

God, the Lover of our souls. In the process, we alienate ourselves from one another. Once the breach is effected, the fatal consequences begin piling up: blame, accusation, hatred, envy, resentment, isolation, death. And so the Cosmic Battle arrives on the home front. It's no wonder that shattered families are one of the hallmarks of a culture in spiritual decline.

Have I considered the many ways in which my relationship with God affects my relationships with those who are closest to me?

For the incomparable blessings of family – brother, sister, parent, spouse, child – I give You thanks, O Lord. Grant that I may never take these precious human relationships for granted. Teach me what it means to show piety at home by caring for the needs of my own household (1 Timothy 5:4, 8). My greatest desire is to seek You with all my heart (Jeremiah 29:13), for I know that in seeking You I will also seek what is best for those who are united to me in bonds of mutual dependency and love.

"THE INTIMATE THREE"

Therefore a man shall leave his father and mother and be joined to his wife, and they shall become one flesh.
Genesis 2:24, NKJV

A little while longer and the world will see Me no more, but you will see Me. Because I live, you will live also. At that day you will know that I am in My Father, and you in Me, and I in you.
John 14:19, 20, NKJV

For no one ever hated his own flesh, but nourishes and cherishes it, just as the Lord does the church. For we are members of His body, of His flesh and of His bones. "For this reason a man shall leave his father and mother and be joined to his wife, and the two shall become one flesh." This is a great mystery, but I speak concerning Christ and the church.
Ephesians 5:29-32, NKJV

Author Charles Williams said that the spiritual and social aspects of man's existence are governed by the principle of "co-inherence" – the mutual delight of finding ourselves *in one another*. His observation bears special application to marriage, the church, and the Christian's personal relationship with the Lord. For it is in the oneness of husband with wife, of Christ with His body, and of God with the individual believer that the mystery of true intimacy is most clearly manifested in the visible world.

Do I realize that personal significance is derived from intimacy with God, my immediate family, and my brothers and sisters in Christ?

You have not left Yourself without witnesses, O Lord. All creation bears the stamp of Your invisible attributes. The heavens declare Your glory. Your wisdom is reflected in the ocean deeps. Reason, order, and symmetry pervade the ways of mankind. Best of all, the joys of true intimacy, hallmark of Your own eternal triune existence, are communicated to us uniquely in the bond of marriage, in the fellowship of the church, and in the mystery of spiritual union with You. Thank You for assuring us that Love is indeed the Lord of heaven and earth.

THE MYSTERY OF GODLINESS

> But He said, "You cannot see My face; for no man
> shall see Me, and live." And the LORD said, "Here is a
> place by Me, and you shall stand on the rock. So it shall
> be, while My glory passes by, that I will put you in the
> cleft of the rock, and will cover you with My hand while
> I pass by. Then I will take away My hand, and you shall
> see My back; but My face shall not be seen."
> **Exodus 33:20-23, NKJV**
>
> By common confession, great is the
> mystery of godliness: He who was revealed in the flesh,
> was vindicated in the Spirit, seen by angels,
> proclaimed among the nations,
> believed on in the world, taken up in glory.
> **1 Timothy 3:16, NASB**

The *social* aspect of man's existence is predicated upon his having been created in the image of a *personal* God. Eternal life, says Jesus, consists in knowing *Him* (John 17:3). But what does this really mean? The answer, of course, is that we don't know. We cannot fully understand; we can only experience, wonder, and worship. God shows us just as much of Himself as we are able to bear. He hides us in the cleft of the Rock, which is Christ, and graciously sheds His glory over us as He passes by.

Does the prospect of actually knowing God in Christ fill me with a sense of awe? Or do I see Christianity as a humdrum religious affair?

_____

_____

_____

_____

I thank You, Father, for the gospel, which is in effect an invitation to partake of Your life and share in the intimacy of the Trinity. I praise You for sending me a Savior whose name is **Immanuel**: God **with** us and **in** us (Isaiah 7:14). My life is hid in You with Christ (Colossians 3:3), and while I cannot fully grasp the implications and ramifications of this astounding mystery, I embrace it as both a present reality and a future hope. This much I know: that when He is revealed, I shall be made like Him, for on that day I shall see Him as He is (1 John 3:2).

And I will ask the Father, and he will give you

another Counselor to be with you forever—the Spirit of truth.

The world cannot accept him, because it neither

sees him nor knows him. But you know him, for he lives

with you and will be in you. ... Because I live, you also will live.

On that day you will realize that I am in my Father,

and you are in me, and I am in you.

John 14:16-20 (NIV)

tour 8

Unio Mystica

am I **Alone**?

THE MYSTERY REVEALED

"But this is the covenant that I will make with the house of Israel after those days, says the LORD: I will put My law in their minds, and write it on their hearts; and I will be their God, and they shall be My people."
Jeremiah 31:33, NKJV

..."Then I will say to those who were not My people, 'You are my people!' And they shall say, 'You are my God!'"
Hosea 2:23, NKJV

... [This is] the mystery which has been hidden from ages and from generations, but now has been revealed to His saints. To them God willed to make known what are the riches of the glory of this mystery among the Gentiles: which is Christ in you, the hope of glory.
Colossians 1:26, 27, NKJV

A "mystery" is not merely an enigma. In the language of the Bible, a "mystery" is *a truth once concealed but now revealed*. Who could have foreseen that the fearsome God of Sinai, who hid His face from Moses and blasted Israel's foes, would one day draw all nations into the circle of His expansive love? Who knew that He would go so far as to come down from the heights and inhabit the individual heart? Yet such is the astonishing truth; for He delights to make His dwelling with the lowly.

Do I appreciate the glorious surprise of God's redemptive work in Christ?

Lord, You have been our dwelling place in all generations. From everlasting to everlasting, You are God (Psalm 90:1). With You there is no variation or shadow of turning (James 1:17); and yet, in the fullness of time, You have chosen to do an entirely new thing in the world. Against all expectation, and contrary to all my merits and deserts, You have seen fit to make Your home within my heart. Purify my mind and make me worthy to serve as a sanctuary of Your holy presence.

IMMANUEL

> Then Samuel took the horn of oil and anointed him
> in the midst of his brothers; and the Spirit of the LORD
> came upon David from that day forward.
> **1 Samuel 16:13, NKJV**
>
> Jesus answered and said to him, "If anyone
> loves Me, he will keep My word; and My Father
> will love him, and We will come to him
> and make Our home with him."
> **John 14:23, NKJV**
>
> Do you not know that your body is the temple
> of the Holy Spirit who is in you, whom you have
> from God, and you are not your own?
> **1 Corinthians 6:19, NKJV**

Isaiah foretold the coming of a Child called *Immanuel*: God with us. The prophet himself probably had no clear idea who that Child would be or how literal the promise of His name would prove to be. Under the Old Covenant, the anointing of God's Spirit was a special grace reserved for unusual saints like David or Elijah. The notion that we, as rank-and-file New Testament believers, can now be indwelt by the personal presence of the infinite, eternal God – *that* is nothing short of revolutionary.

question

Have I grasped the deeper implications of the gospel promise: "Christ in me, the hope of glory"? (Colossians 1:27)

response

prayer

What does it mean, Lord, to say that I – not merely in my spiritual "inner" being, but in my physical body – have become a temple, a dwelling place for Your Holy Spirit? How is it possible that I, a mere human being, can be joined to the Alpha and Omega, the Creator of the universe, in bonds of intimate fellowship and love? By faith I confess that I **have** the Spirit of Christ. If I did not have His Spirit, I would have no part in Him at all (Romans 8:9). I know that this is true, though I do not claim to understand it. Fill me with an appropriate attitude of reverence and awe.

"THE PILLAR AND GROUND OF THE TRUTH"

"I will set My tabernacle among you, and My soul
shall not abhor you. I will walk among you and
be your God, and you shall be My people."
Leviticus 26:11, 12, NKJV

..."The kingdom of God is not coming with signs to
be observed; nor will they say, 'Look, here it is!' or, 'There
it is!' For behold, the kingdom of God is in your midst."
Luke 17:20, 21, NASB

Now, therefore, you are no longer strangers and
foreigners, but fellow citizens with the saints and
members of the household of God, having been built
on the foundation of the apostles and prophets,
Jesus Christ Himself being the chief cornerstone,
in whom the whole building, being fitted together,
grows into a holy temple in the Lord, in whom
you also are being built together for a
dwelling place of God in the Spirit.
Ephesians 2:19-22, NKJV

It is true that the Holy Spirit lives in the individual believer. But this isn't

the end of the story, for individual believers are also the "living stones" out of which God builds a great "spiritual house" (1 Peter 2:5) in which to compound the manifestation of His power and presence. This house is the church, the Body of Christ. Paul calls it "the pillar and ground of the truth" (1 Timothy 3:15). No amount of "solo spirituality" can ever take its place, for in this case, the whole is far greater than the sum of the parts.

question

Do I understand the role of the church in God's redemptive plan?

response

prayer

Thank You, God, for giving me a place among Your people and grafting me into the living Body of Christ. What a blessing it is to stand in the midst of the family and call You **"Abba, Father"** (Romans 8:15)! I know that my brothers and sisters are essential to my spiritual health and well-being; I confess that the eye cannot say to the hand, "I have no need of you" (1 Corinthians 12:21). I realize, too, that the bond we share is vital to the success of Your mission in the world. Make me a faithful servant, not only of Jesus Christ, but also of His glorious bride, the church.

"THAT THEY MAY BE ONE"

Behold, how good and how pleasant it is
for brethren to dwell together in unity!
Psalm 133:1, NKJV

"I do not pray for these alone, but also for those who
will believe in Me through their word; that they all
may be one, as You, Father, are in Me and I in You;
that they also may be one in Us, that the world
may believe that You sent Me."
John 17:20, 21, NKJV

There is one body and one Spirit, just as you were
called in one hope of your calling; one Lord, one faith,
one baptism; one God and Father of all, who is
above all, and through all, and in you all.
Ephesians 4:4-6, NKJV

One phrase recurs with striking regularity throughout the words of Jesus
and the language of the New Testament: *"one another." Reciprocity*
of love, service, and submission is central to the meaning of the gospel
and the life of the church. Again and again the apostles urge believers to

live in unity, put others' interests first, and *be of the same mind in the Lord* (Philippians 4:2). The message is clear: *oneness* with God implies *oneness* with *one another*. It's all part of a single redemptive process.

Am I content to live in my own little world with my favorite Christian friends? Or do I actively seek the unity of the larger Body of Christ?

Jesus, You said that there is only one way for the world to know that the gospel is true and that we as believers are genuinely Your disciples: we must love one another as You have loved us (John 13:35; 17:23). We must lift the winsome banner of life in lived community. We must care for one another in such a way that skeptics will be forced to reevaluate our message. I realize that, through selfishness, I have contributed to the ugly divisions that plague Your people. Heal Your church, I pray. Make us one in the Spirit. And let the healing process begin with me.

THE SEARCH FOR SIGNIFICANCE

When Haman saw that Mordecai did not bow
or pay him homage, Haman was filled with wrath.
Esther 3:5, NKJV

Why do you spend money for what is not bread,
and your wages for what does not satisfy? Listen
carefully to Me, and eat what is good, and
let your soul delight itself in abundance.
Isaiah 55:2, NKJV

..."I swore an oath to you and entered into a covenant
with you, and you became Mine," says the LORD God. ...
"But you trusted in your own beauty, played the harlot
because of your fame, and poured out your harlotry on
everyone passing by who would have it."
Ezekiel 16:8, 15, NKJV

"But seek first the kingdom of God and His
righteousness, and all these things shall be added to you."
Matthew 6:33, NKJV

What divides us from God and one another? The answer is simple: *self.* So
overpowering was Haman's lust for significance that he was compelled to

kill any man who refused to grovel before him. Israel preferred her *own* glory to the love of her heavenly Husband. But the quest for self isn't merely hollow – it's *self-destructive*. To live in a cage of envy and pride is to cut oneself off from the heart of intimacy. There is only one path to fulfillment and joy, and *it* leads through the narrow gate of *self-denial*.

Do I see the speck of selfish ambition in my own eye?

Grant me eyes to see beyond myself, O Lord. Help me to put personal interest aside and discern the face of Christ in the faces of the people around me. Whatever I do to one of the least of these, **Your** brethren, I am doing it to **You** (Matthew 25:40), for the Scripture declares that both He who sanctifies and those who are being sanctified are all one (Hebrews 2:11). Enable me to love You by loving others and in so doing to find my niche in Your eternal plan. There is no prize worth gaining, no lasting significance to be found, outside the circle of Your all-inclusive love.

THE ORIGIN OF NATIONS

"He makes nations great, and destroys them;
He enlarges nations, and guides them."
Job 12:23, NKJV

"Blessed be the name of God forever and ever,
for wisdom and might are His, and He changes
the times and the seasons; He removes kings and
raises up kings; He gives wisdom to the wise and
knowledge to those who have understanding."
Daniel 2:20, 21, NKJV

"[God] has made from one blood every nation
of men to dwell on all the face of the earth,
and has determined their preappointed times and
the boundaries of their dwellings ..."
Acts 17:26, NKJV

As a creature uniquely shaped in the image of God, man mirrors his Creator's nature in a number of different ways. Human life is incomplete, for instance, unless it is *shared* and *communal*. Similarly, this corporate life, if it is to function smoothly, must be *orderly* and *structured*. Thus it happens that wherever we look, we see people confronting the challenges of life in *organic* and *organized* groups – everything from family to tribe to nation-state. This, too, is a direct reflection of the divine character.

Do I recognize the imprint of God's nature upon every aspect of the social realm – national and political as well as spiritual and ecclesiastical?

_____

_____

_____

_____

_____

The earth is Yours, Lord, and the fullness thereof, the world and those who dwell in it (Psalm 24:1). I thank You that You have devised a perfect plan, not only for my personal fulfillment, nor merely for the advancement of Your church, but for the well-being of every people and ethnic group on earth. You cause the sun to rise on the evil and on the good. You send the rain on the just and on the unjust (Matthew 5:45). In the same way, You order the life of the nations so that, in following Your will, men may find peace and come to a deeper understanding of Your love (Acts 17:27).

STRUCTURES AND STANDARDS

It is an abomination for kings to commit wickedness,
for a throne is established by righteousness.
Proverbs 16:12, NKJV

Take away the dross from silver, and it will
go to the silversmith for jewelry. Take away the
wicked from before the king, and his throne
will be established in righteousness.
Proverbs 25:4, 5, NKJV

Therefore I exhort first of all that supplications, prayers,
intercessions, and giving of thanks be made for all men,
for kings and all who are in authority, that we may lead
a quiet and peaceable life in all godliness and reverence.
1 Timothy 2:1, 2, NKJV

Nations, states, and communities cannot be peaceful and productive unless they are organized with reference to some higher standard of order and structure. This is where the **communal** aspects of human life intersect with the **ethical** implications of the **Imago Dei**. It's the origin of the concept of *law*: a transcendent principle that guides and directs the actions of every member of society, from servant to senator to king. Precisely *what* that law says – and *whose* it is – makes all the difference in the world.

Do I understand the importance of maintaining high ethical standards in the life of the community and in my relationships with others?

God, Your grace is the cornerstone of all goodness, decency, and Truth. You have said that righteousness exalts a nation (Proverbs 14:34), but how can Your people stand if that sure foundation should be destroyed (Psalm 11:3)? Keep us, I pray, from such calamity. Let us shine as lights in the world for You (Philippians 2:15). Grant that there may be no famine of hearing Your words in our land (Amos 8:11), but rather a fresh turning of hearts toward Your mercy and love. Be exalted, O God, above the heavens; let Your glory be above all the earth (Psalm 57:11)!

The king's heart is in the hand of the Lord;

he directs it like a watercourse wherever he pleases.

Proverbs 21:1 (NIV)

tour **9**

The State

whose **Law**?

AUTHORITY DELEGATED

For the Scripture says to the Pharaoh, "For this
very purpose I have raised you up, that I may show
My power in you, and that My name may
be declared in all the earth."
Romans 9:17, NKJV

Let every soul be subject to the governing authorities.
For there is no authority except from God, and the
authorities that exist are appointed by God.
Romans 13:1, NKJV

And He has on His robe and on His thigh a name
written: KING OF KINGS AND LORD OF LORDS.
Revelation 19:16, NKJV

If the nations owe their existence to God, and if the laws by which they
are governed depend upon His truth, it follows that He must take a strong
personal interest in the administration of their day-to-day affairs. This
is what the apostle means when he says that there is no authority except
from God. Whether they know it or not, the people who stand at the top of

the social and political pyramid are acting as His appointed delegates. The very *concept* of authority is grounded in the reality of His sovereign will.

Do I respect human authorities as representatives of the sovereign Lord?

Father, You are the great King from whom the whole family in heaven and earth takes its name (Ephesians 3:14). The rulers of this world are only tools in Your hand, instruments through whom You accomplish Your sovereign purposes (Isaiah 45:4); You turn their hearts whichever way You wish (Proverbs 21:1). Help me to honor You by respecting the dignity of their office. Teach me to cooperate with them in the doing of Your will. My desire is to adorn the doctrine of my Savior in all things by adopting a Christlike attitude of submission and fidelity (Titus 2:10).

AUTHORITY AND ACCOUNTABILITY

Divination is on the lips of the king; his mouth
must not transgress in judgment.
Proverbs 16:10, NKJV

"I have also given you what you have not asked: both
riches and honor, so that there shall not be anyone like
you among the kings all your days. So if you walk in My
ways, to keep My statutes and My commandments, as
your father David walked, then I will lengthen your days."
1 Kings 3:13, 14, NKJV

So on a set day Herod, arrayed in royal apparel, sat
on his throne and gave an oration to them. And the
people kept shouting, "The voice of a god and not of
a man!" Then immediately an angel of the Lord struck
him, because he did not give glory to God.
And he was eaten by worms and died.
Acts 12:21-23, NKJV

"I am the state." This grandiose claim is attributed to Louis XIV, France's
illustrious "Sun King," who is also reported to have said, "It is legal

because I wish it." Apocryphal or not, Louis' boasting is characteristic of human authorities who choose to disconnect from the eternal source of their temporal power. As the Lord reminded Solomon, even an emperor is accountable to the King of all kings. Rulers who forget this lesson are among humanity's most fearsome enemies.

Do I keep the power and authority of human rulers in proper perspective?

Convince me, Lord, of Your absolute sovereignty over the affairs of humankind. In all of my relationships and all of my dealings with the wider world, whether as parent, child, employer, employee, citizen, or member of Your church, let me never forget that You stand at the pinnacle of every authoritative hierarchy. Ultimately, all owe their allegiance and obedience to You; for You alone are the Lord, and there is no God besides You (Isaiah 45:5).

GOD AND CAESAR

> But the midwives feared God, and did not
> do as the king of Egypt commanded them,
> but saved the male children alive.
> **Exodus 1:17, NKJV**
>
> ...He said to them, "Whose image and inscription
> is this?" They said to Him, "Caesar's." And Jesus
> answered and said to them, "Render to Caesar the
> things that are Caesar's, and to God the things that are
> God's." And they marveled at Him.
> **Mark 12:16, 17, NKJV**
>
> But Peter and the other apostles answered and said:
> "We ought to obey God rather than men."
> **Acts 5:29, NKJV**

Jesus' famous words convey a message so subtle that it is often overlooked: *not everything belongs to Caesar.* Rulers who overstep the bounds – who disregard ethical standards and unjustly seize control of social spheres outside their jurisdiction – are evidence of state authority run amok. By refusing to answer the Pharisees directly, Christ raised the stakes and threw the ball back in *their* court; as if He were to say, "Go figure out what belongs to Caesar and what truly belongs to God."

Am I discerning enough to know when Caesar and Christ are in conflict? Do I have the courage to stay true to the higher authority?

Lord, grant that I may become not so much a rebel to the wrong as an unswerving devotee of the Truth. When confronted with clear choices between loyalty to Your kingdom and love for the kingdoms of this world, help me to take Your side without flinching or looking back (Luke 9:62). Make me like Shadrach, Meshach, and Abednego, who were brave enough to look the king of Babylon in the eye and say, "O king, we do not serve your gods, nor will we worship the gold image which you have set up" (Daniel 3:18). Let me serve my country by loving You with all my heart.

PATHOLOGICAL POWER

Why do the nations rage, and the people plot a vain thing? The kings of the earth set themselves, and the rulers take counsel together, against the LORD and against His Anointed, saying, "Let us break Their bonds in pieces and cast away Their cords from us."
Psalm 2:1-3, NKJV

[Nebuchadnezzar] spoke, saying, "Is not this great Babylon, that I have built for a royal dwelling by my mighty power and for the honor of my majesty?"
Daniel 4:30, NKJV

Then Herod, when he saw that he was deceived by the wise men, was exceedingly angry; and he sent forth and put to death all the male children who were in Bethlehem and in all its districts, from two years old and under, according to the time which he had determined from the wise men.
Matthew 2:16, NKJV

... for he [the ruler] does not bear the sword in vain ...
Romans 13:4, NKJV

reflection

To the state has been delegated the power of the sword; and, as Paul tells us in Romans 13, it does not wield this power "to no effect." Precisely **what** the "effect" will be is entirely dependent upon the ruler's conception of his own position. If he is mindful of his responsibility to the Delegating Authority, the outcome can be order, justice, and peace. But if he sees himself as a self-made potentate, the results can be disastrous: oppression, tyranny, infanticide, slaughter, and the death of humanity itself.

Have I seriously pondered the frightening prospect of power and authority divorced from the righteousness of God? *question*

response

prayer

O God, it is only by Your providence that we are preserved in peace and safety for a single day in such a world as this (John Newton). I thank You for the gift of Your protecting grace. My prayer, like David's, is that we may be permitted in every situation and circumstance to fall into the sheltering hollow of Your almighty hand, for Your mercies are great; but do not let us fall into the hand of man (2 Samuel 24:14).

ANOTHER KING

And the Lord said to Samuel, "Heed the voice of the people in all they say to you; for they have not rejected you, but they have rejected Me, that I should not reign over them."
1 Samuel 8:7, NKJV

Jesus answered, "My kingdom is not of this world. If My kingdom were of this world, My servants would fight, so that I should not be delivered to the Jews; but now My kingdom is not from here."
John 18:36, NKJV

...They dragged Jason and some brethren to the rulers of the city, crying out, "These who have turned the world upside down have come here too. Jason has harbored them, and these are all acting contrary to the decrees of Caesar, saying there is another king – Jesus."
Acts 17:6, 7, NKJV

Christians are called to live peaceably in this world and to submit to human rulers insofar as it is possible to do so without violating conscience or transgressing the laws of God. But they must never forget that there is another King and that they are subjects of a different kingdom. In essence, the church is an *outpost* or *embassy* of that other realm. And as ambassadors, believers have been given the prophetic task of holding the nations accountable to the standards of eternal truth.

Do I understand my responsibility as an ambassador for Christ living on foreign soil?

Father, may I never lose sight of the church's creed in its earliest and most primitive form: "Christ is king! Jesus is Lord!" (1 Corinthians 12:3). Remind me daily of the revolutionary implications of these simple words. All authority in heaven and on earth belongs to You (Matthew 28:18). My role as a subject of the King is to participate in the process of spreading the Word and making disciples in every nation. Make me a faithful and diligent exponent of that saving message: "We implore you on Christ's behalf, be reconciled to God" (2 Corinthians 5:20).

TOWARD AN IDEAL

The king's favor is toward a wise servant, but
his wrath is against him who causes shame.
Proverbs 14:35, NKJV

It is an abomination for kings to commit wickedness,
for a throne is established by righteousness.
Proverbs 16:12, NKJV

For rulers are not a terror to good works, but to evil.
Do you want to be unafraid of the authority? Do what is
good, and you will have praise from the same. For he is
God's minister to you for good. But if you do evil,
be afraid; for he does not bear the sword in vain; for
he is God's minister, an avenger to execute wrath
on him who practices evil.
Romans 13:3, 4, NKJV

According to Scripture, human government is an agency appointed by God
on earth to administer justice, punish evil, and foster goodness among its
citizens or subjects. What would happen if a group of people intentionally
set out to build a system of government based on this biblical model?

Would it work? What would it look like? These are questions well worth pondering, for at least once in the history of the world – on the shores of North America – the experiment has been seriously attempted.

question

Do I appreciate the ethical and theological significance of the bold venture undertaken by America's Founding Fathers?

response

_____

_____

_____

_____

prayer

I thank You, Lord, for the courage and intentionality of men who were not afraid to apply transcendent truths to the nuts-and-bolts business of running a country and providing for the common welfare. Such is the vision and philosophy upon which the American nation has been founded. It is a vision that Christians can enthusiastically endorse, for as You are, so also are we in this world (1 John 4:17). We are not called to keep Your eternal principles locked up in theological books but rather to put them to use in everyday life. Make me a part of that life-giving process.

GOVERNMENT AND CULTURE

Blessed is the nation whose God is the Lord…
Psalm 33:12, NKJV

Where there is no vision, the people perish…
Proverbs 29:18, KJV

But everyone shall sit under his vine and under
his fig tree, and no one shall make them afraid; for
the mouth of the Lord of hosts has spoken. For all
people walk each in the name of his god, but we will
walk in the name of the Lord our God forever and ever.
Micah 4:4, 5, NKJV

"A good man out of the good treasure of his heart
brings forth good things, and an evil man out
of the evil treasure brings forth evil things."
Matthew 12:35, NKJV

Out of the heart – the principle is as valid of society as a whole as it
is of the individual. Though divinely appointed, the implementation of
government is a thoroughly human invention; and, like other human

artifacts, it reflects the attitudes and values of the culture that produces it. The unique thing about the American system is that it arose in a culture saturated with the biblical worldview. This is why John Adams could say that it is "wholly inadequate" for the governing of any but "a moral and religious people."

Have I considered the organic connections among spirituality, culture, and the form of the state in any given society?

God, I understand that You are sovereign over every aspect of my personal existence **and** the communal life I share with other human beings. I know that there is and must always be a direct connection between the quality of that life and the degree to which we as a people have individually and collectively internalized the principles of Your unchanging Truth. Salt is good, but if the salt loses its flavor, how can it be seasoned? Help me to have salt in myself and thus to contribute to the "salting" of society as a whole (Mark 9:50).

Remember the height from which you have fallen! Repent and do the things you did at first. If you do not repent, I will come to you and remove your lampstand from its place.

Revelation 2:5 (NIV)

tour **10**

American Experiment

stepping **Stones**

FOUNDATIONS

"Therefore whoever hears these sayings of Mine,
and does them, I will liken him to a wise man who built
his house on the rock: and the rain descended, the
floods came, and the winds blew and beat on that
house; and it did not fall, for it was founded on the rock."
Matthew 7:24, 25, NKJV

According to the grace of God which was
given to me, as a wise master builder I have laid the
foundation, and another builds on it.
But let each one take heed how he builds on it.
1 Corinthians 3:10, NKJV

The most important feature of any building is the part we don't see. If
the *foundation* is flawed, the superstructure eventually crumbles; if it is
sound, the house holds together as a beautiful and harmonious whole. The
foundations of the American system of government were intentionally laid
in the solid rock of Truth – "the laws of nature and of nature's God." But
this experiment, unique in the history of statecraft, can succeed only to
the extent that its foundation is thoughtfully and carefully maintained.

Am I aware of the importance of the theological and philosophical underpinnings of American democracy? Will I work to restore them?

I know, O Lord, that all nations are as nothing before You and that You count them as less than nothing and worthless (Isaiah 40:17). At the same time, I believe that You will not fail to bless **any** people who honor Your Truth and walk in Your ways, for You remain faithful and cannot deny Yourself (2 Timothy 2:13). Demonstrate that faithfulness, I pray, by granting continued success to those nations who honor You.

TO PRESERVE AND MAINTAIN

"And these words which I command you today shall
be in your heart. You shall teach them diligently
to your children, and shall talk of them when you sit
in your house, when you walk by the way, when you
lie down, and when you rise up. You shall bind them as
a sign on your hand, and they shall be as frontlets
between your eyes. You shall write them on
the doorposts of your house and on your gates."
Deuteronomy 6:6-9, NKJV

"This Book of the Law shall not depart from your
mouth, but you shall meditate in it day and night, that
you may observe to do according to all that is written in
it. For then you will make your way prosperous,
and then you will have good success."
Joshua 1:8, NKJV

You therefore, my son, be strong in the grace that is
in Christ Jesus. And the things that you have heard
from me among many witnesses, commit these
to faithful men who will be able to teach others also.
2 Timothy 2:1, 2, NKJV

The value of education is implicit in the biblical worldview. We all have to discover God's timeless truths for ourselves. The blessings of righteousness, piety, and freedom are not necessarily obvious to the flawed perception of fallen man; they must be relearned and experienced anew in every generation. We dare not take anything for granted, for as William Bradford observed, we alone are to blame if we forfeit our forefathers' hard-won achievements through inattention and sloth.

Am I actively involved in the process of preserving a godly heritage and passing it on to the next generation?

I thank You, Father, for the heritage with which You have blessed me – for people who went before to do the hard work of laying cultural, social, and political foundations grounded upon the bedrock of Your eternal law. Humanly speaking, I don't know where we would be today without their heroic efforts; they have left us a gift of incalculable worth. Help me to participate in the process of passing that gift along to future generations. Enable me to teach and mentor others who desperately need to know the Truth (Hebrews 5:12). I can aspire to no higher calling.

FAT AND FORGETFUL

> But Jeshurun grew fat and kicked; you grew fat, you
> grew thick, you are obese! Then he forsook God
> who made him, and scornfully esteemed
> the Rock of his salvation.
> **Deuteronomy 32:15, NKJV**
>
> When they had pasture, they were filled; they were filled
> and their heart was exalted; therefore they forgot Me.
> **Hosea 13:6, NKJV**
>
> I marvel that you are turning away so soon from Him who
> called you in the grace of Christ, to a different gospel...
> **Galatians 1:6, NKJV**

"Prosperity," wrote English Puritan John Owen, "has slain the foolish and wounded the wise."[7] His words bear a perennial relevance to the human situation. Again and again man forgets his Maker and scorns His priceless gifts – not only from generation to generation, but from year to year, day to day, and hour to hour. Ironically, this forgetfulness tends to be most pervasive at those moments when temporal blessings are most abundant. Such is the fickleness and instability of the human heart.

Do I recognize the dangers of luxury, affluence, and pride, not only in American society and the world at large, but also in my own spiritual life?

_____

_____

_____

_____

_____

God, You have said that the heart is deceitful above all things and desperately wicked (Jeremiah 17:9). If this is true on an individual level, how great is the potential for darkness when human hearts are banded together in the combined life of societies, nations, and states! I am afraid that the heart of my country has been taken captive by the deceitfulness of riches (Mark 4:19) – that in the midst of so many blessings, secured through adherence to the principles of Your Word, we have somehow forgotten You. Have mercy upon us, O Lord, and save us from ourselves!

---

[7] John Owen, "Of Temptation," in *The Works of John Owen*, vol. VI (Edinburgh: The Banner of Truth Trust, 1967), 112.

REMEMBER, REPENT, RETURN

Come, and let us return to the LORD; for He has torn,
but He will heal us; He has stricken, but He will bind us
up. After two days He will revive us; on the third day
He will raise us up, that we may live in His sight.
Hosea 6:1, 2, NKJV

"I will arise and go to my father, and will say to him,
'Father, I have sinned against heaven and before you ...'"
Luke 15:18, NKJV

"... I have this against you, that you have left your
first love. Remember therefore from where you have
fallen; repent and do the first works, or else I will
come to you quickly and remove your lampstand
from its place – unless you repent."
Revelation 2:4, 5, NKJV

There is only one cure for the malaise of ethical and spiritual forgetfulness:
one has to take the trouble to *remember*. *Repentance* – the 180-degree
turn, the deliberate reversal of harmful attitudes and behaviors – was one
of the central themes of Jesus' preaching. In God's economy, *returning* is

always an option. It can happen in America today. But it will happen only if Christian people are willing to spearhead the movement with an attitude of compassion, humility, and love.

question

Am I concerned about the spiritual well-being of my country? Do I care enough to become engaged in the battle for her soul?

response

_____

_____

_____

_____

prayer

Grant me grace, O Lord, to speak the truth in love (Ephesians 4:15). Make me swift to hear, slow to speak, slow to wrath (James 1:19) – readier to search my own heart than to point the finger of blame at others. It is true that our nation has in many ways drifted far from its original moorings, but I confess that the key to solving this problem lies not in angry confrontations but rather in the cleansing of my own soul and the conversion of my own heart. Lead me along the pathway of repentance and renewal in accord with Your great mercy and love.

STEPPING STONES

"I do not pray for these alone, but also for those
who will believe in Me through their word ..."
John 17:20, NKJV

Who then is Paul, and who is Apollos,
but ministers through whom you believed,
as the Lord gave to each one? I planted, Apollos
watered, but God gave the increase.
1 Corinthians 3:5, 6, NKJV

Now, therefore, you are no longer strangers and
foreigners, but fellow citizens with the saints and
members of the household of God, having been built
on the foundation of the apostles and prophets,
Jesus Christ Himself being the chief cornerstone.
Ephesians 2:19, 20, NKJV

According to Governor Bradford, the Pilgrim fathers came to North
America in hopes of "laying some good foundation ... for the propagating
and advancing of the Gospel ..." At the very least, they trusted that their
efforts might become "stepping stones unto others for the performing of

so great a work."[8] *We* are the heirs of their hopes; *we* are the "others" for whom the "stepping stones" were laid. Our task is to build wisely on this foundation, and in so doing to light a candle for future generations.

Do I appreciate the solemn responsibility and unparalleled opportunity I have been given as a Christian and a citizen of a nation built on Christian principles and aspirations?

God of the ages, You teach us in Your Word that our relationship with You is constantly new and renewable. We dare not place our confidence in the righteousness and zeal of preceding generations. Instead, we must go forward with Christ our King before us. It is not enough to claim Abraham as our father – we must **do** the works of Abraham (John 8:39) and then move on to the **greater works** that Jesus promised we would accomplish in His name (John 14:12). Such is the calling You have laid upon us in this generation. Help us to embrace it with faith, hope, and courage.

[8] William Bradford, *Of Plimouth Plantation, 1620-1647* (New York: Modern Library College Editions, 1981), 26.

"TO WORK THE WORKS OF GOD"

Then they said to Him, "What shall we do, that we may work the works of God?" Jesus answered and said to them, "This is the work of God, that you believe in Him whom He sent."
John 6:28, 29, NKJV

Now if anyone builds on this foundation with gold, silver, precious stones, wood, hay, straw, each one's work will become clear; for the Day will declare it, because it will be revealed by fire; and the fire will test each one's work, of what sort it is. If anyone's work which he has built on it endures, he will receive a reward.
1 Corinthians 3:12-14, NKJV

Thus also faith by itself, if it does not have works, is dead.
James 2:17, NKJV

In the midst of theological debates about faith and works, we can easily lose sight of a vital spiritual truth: God has put each one of us in this world to *do* something. Jesus Himself "went about doing good" (Acts

10:38), and the deeds He performed were essential to the message He proclaimed. Through faith in Him we, too, can play a part in the coming of the kingdom. For when we truly belong to Christ, everything about us – our works and actions as well as our beliefs – tends to the glory of God.

Do I understand the Christian life as a labor of love?

Lord, You sent Your Son to work, strive, achieve, suffer, and die on our behalf. By His example, You have demonstrated the truth of Fyodor Dostoevsky's observation that "active love is labor and fortitude." You are the God who made the world (Genesis 1:1), who diligently attends to the smallest of my concerns (Job 23:14), and who never slumbers nor sleeps (Psalm 121:4). Thank You for giving me tasks to accomplish and for calling me to be a co-laborer with You (1 Corinthians 3:9).

CREATIVE ENERGY

Now King Solomon sent and brought Huram from Tyre.
He was the son of a widow from the tribe of Naphtali,
and his father was a man of Tyre, a bronze worker;
he was filled with wisdom and understanding and skill
in working with all kinds of bronze work. So he came
to King Solomon and did all his work.
1 Kings 7:13, 14, NKJV

"When He assigned to the sea its limit, so that
the waters would not transgress His command, when
He marked out the foundations of the earth, then I
[Wisdom] was beside Him as a master craftsman; and I
was daily His delight, rejoicing always before Him ..."
Proverbs 8:29, 30, NKJV

"By this My Father is glorified, that you bear much fruit;
so you will be My disciples."
John 15:8, NKJV

Like Solomon of old, the King of Creation has work to do, and He is

looking for craftsmen to help Him do it. All creativity derives from Him, for without Him nothing was made that was made, and the wisdom, facility, and skill required to effect any good work are gifts that He alone can bestow. It is in His nature to design, invent, and proliferate beautiful and useful things. As people made in His image, we are appointed to produce similar fruits by drawing on His energy and abiding in His love.

Have I known the joy of impacting my world as an enterprising co-worker with God?

You, O Lord, are the Father of lights, and all good gifts come down to us from Your hand (James 1:17). You have given me the privilege, not only of worshiping You in the beauty of holiness (Psalm 29:2), but also of embellishing Your world with works worthy of Your loveliness and grace. Reveal to me the unique abilities with which You have gifted me. Grant me opportunities to use them. Help me to find my niche in the ongoing task of adorning the marvelous temple of Your creation.

Six days you shall labor and do all your work,

but the seventh day is a Sabbath to the Lᴏʀᴅ your God. ...

For in six days the Lᴏʀᴅ made the heavens and

the earth, the sea, and all that is in them, but he rested

on the seventh day. Therefore the Lᴏʀᴅ blessed

the Sabbath day and made it holy.

Exodus 20:9-11 (NIV)

tour **11**

Labor

created to **Create**

POSSESSION AND PERSONHOOD

Then God said, "Let Us make man in Our image, according to Our likeness; let them have dominion over the fish of the sea, over the birds of the air, and over the cattle, over all the earth and over every creeping thing that creeps on the earth."
Genesis 1:26, NKJV

"You shall not steal."
Exodus 20:15, NKJV

"While it remained, was it not your own? And after it was sold, was it not in your own control?..."
Acts 5:4, NKJV

The principles of *ownership* and *dominion* are basic to the meaning of personhood. Man controls, develops, and cares for his *things* precisely because he is made in the image of God. What's mine is mine to dispose of as I will; to take it from me is to strike a blow at the very core of my humanity. This passion for possession is an incentive to all kinds of action, labor, sacrifice, and striving. And in this power of disposal lies a vast potential for either tremendous good or incalculable evil.

Have I examined the place of personal property in God's design for human life and the sphere of labor?

_____

_____

_____

_____

_____

_____

_____

For the many rich gifts You have poured out on me, Lord – possessions both material and spiritual, intellectual, emotional, and relational – I offer You praise and thanks. All I am and all I have I owe to You. As Your child, I have been granted the privilege of partaking of the goodness of Your creation (Genesis 1:28, 31). Help me to understand and appreciate the grace You have delegated to me as a co-regent and co-possessor of Your world.

HELD IN TRUST

What is man that You are mindful of him, and
the son of man that You visit him? For You have made
him a little lower than the angels, and You have
crowned him with glory and honor. You have made him
to have dominion over the works of Your hands ...
Psalm 8:4-6, NKJV

The earth is the LORD's, and all its fullness,
the world and those who dwell therein.
Psalm 24:1, NKJV

"For she does not know that it was I who gave her
the grain, the new wine, and the oil, and lavished
on her silver and gold, which they used for Baal."
Hosea 2:8, NASB

...What do you have that you did not receive?
Now if you did indeed receive it, why do you
boast as if you had not received it?
1 Corinthians 4:7, NKJV

Human ownership rights are not absolute. Instead, they are contingent upon the goodwill of the One who delegates them. God is the owner of *everything*; we are mere stewards who have been assigned the task of cultivating **His** property with an eye to **His** interests and concerns. It is all too easy to forget this truth and to boast of our own achievements, as the Corinthians did, or to abuse and misuse the gifts of God, as the people of Israel did. Against such folly we must be constantly on our guard.

Do I understand my role as a steward entrusted with the care of God's possessions and goods?

You, Father God, are Master and Possessor of all things. I acknowledge You, not only as my personal Savior, but also as King of kings and Lord of lords (Revelation 19:16). There is nothing in the entire universe that falls outside the range of Your ownership and jurisdiction; every beast of the forest is Yours, and the cattle on a thousand hills (Psalm 50:10). Make me mindful of my duties and responsibilities as a steward of Your great wealth. Like Moses, let me dwell in Your house as a faithful servant, offering testimony in all I do to the wonder of Your goodness and grace.

TENDING THE GARDEN

> Then the LORD God took the man and put him
> in the garden of Eden to tend and keep it.
> **Genesis 2:15, NKJV**
>
> Then Moses called Bezalel and Oholiab and every skillful
> person in whom the LORD had put skill, everyone whose
> heart stirred him, to come to the work to perform it.
> **Exodus 36:2, NASB**
>
> For we are His workmanship, created in
> Christ Jesus for good works, which God prepared
> beforehand that we should walk in them.
> **Ephesians 2:10, NKJV**
>
> But be doers of the word, and not
> hearers only, deceiving yourselves.
> **James 1:22, NKJV**

Scripture describes human beings as both "workers" ("doers") *and*
"workmanship" – both "poets" (greek *poietai*) *and* "a poem" (greek *poiema*).
In the words of J. R. R. Tolkien, "We make … by the law in which we're

made."[9] This is the meaning behind the deep human impulse to shape, tame, organize, and improve. As Tolkien explains, we are "sub-creators," assisting God in "the effoliation and multiple enrichment of creation." Such is the mind-boggling significance of the work we do in this world.

Am I aware of the privilege I have been granted as a "doer" and "maker" made in the image of the Creator of all things?

Thank You, Lord, for assigning me a significant place in creation and giving me meaningful work to do. It is reassuring to know that, in Christ, my labor is not in vain (1 Corinthians 15:58) – that when I stay faithful to Your will, abounding in Your work, the apparent emptiness of human endeavor (Ecclesiastes 2:22, 23) vanishes like a bad dream in the morning light. It is in seeking Your kingdom that we gain all things (Matthew 6:33), and within the circle of Your blessing and grace, it is indeed good to eat, drink, and enjoy the fruits of our labor (Ecclesiastes 2:24).

---

[9] J.R.R. Tolkien, "On Fairy Stories", in *The Tolkien Reader,* (New York: Ballantine Books, 1966), 54, 73.

BLESSED OR CURSED?

> Then God blessed them, and God said to them,
> "Be fruitful and multiply; fill the earth and subdue it ..."
> **Genesis 1:28, NKJV**

> "...Cursed is the ground for your sake;
> in toil you shall eat of it all the days of your life."
> **Genesis 3:17, NKJV**

> For the earnest expectation of the creation eagerly
> waits for the revealing of the sons of God. For the
> creation was subjected to futility, not willingly, but
> because of Him who subjected it in hope; because the
> creation itself also will be delivered from the bondage of
> corruption into the glorious liberty of the children of God.
> **Romans 8:19-21, NKJV**

Man's call to be an "effoliator" of God's garden predates his original act
of disobedience and sin. The **work** (hebrew **mela'chah**) he was given to
do in the garden, like that of the angels themselves (**mal'achim**), was
delegated to him as an aspect of his role as the Image-bearer image bearer;
whereas the **travail** (**'itstsabon**) that now besets his best efforts reflects

the groaning of a cursed and fallen creation. But the curse will be removed and all good work redeemed at the appearing of the Deliverer from on high.

question

Do I see my work as a blessing or a curse?

response

prayer

O God, lead me into a deeper and fuller understanding of Your Word's teaching on the subject of labor. Revolutionize my attitude toward work. You have instructed me to be diligent, to live quietly, to attend to business, and to work with my hands, that I may lack nothing and represent You faithfully in an unbelieving world (1 Thessalonians 4:11, 12). You have also assured me that there is profit in all labor (Proverbs 14:23) and that a man who excels in his work will stand before kings (Proverbs 22:29). Reveal to me the joy of this high and blessed calling.

GOODNESS, TRUTH, AND BEAUTY

"And you shall make holy garments for Aaron
your brother, for glory and for beauty."
Exodus 28:2, NKJV

...Let the beauty of the LORD our God be upon us,
and establish the work of our hands for us ...
Psalm 90:17, NKJV

Finally, brethren, whatever things are true, whatever
things are noble, whatever things are just, whatever
things are pure, whatever things are lovely, whatever
things are of good report, if there is any virtue and if there
is anything praiseworthy—meditate on these things.
Philippians 4:8, NKJV

Every good gift and every perfect gift is from above,
and comes down from the Father of lights, with whom
there is no variation or shadow of turning. Of His own
will He brought us forth by the word of truth, that we
might be a kind of firstfruits of His creatures.
James 1:17, 18, NKJV

Men and women, like the God who created them, are artists by nature. In spite of the Fall, "we make *still* by the law in which we're made" (Tolkien), and that law says that good work is not just practical or utilitarian; it is also *beautiful*. As an element of the divine nature, beauty, like righteousness and truth, is measured by an absolute standard. Let the critics say what they will: a sunset will always be lovelier than a crushed cigarette box – at least in the *real* world that God has made.

Do I recognize God's sovereignty over the creative arts? Am I concerned to bring them into conformity with His standards of beauty and truth?

For the beauty of the earth, the glory of the skies, the miracle of tree and flower, the light of sun and stars, I give You thanks, O Lord. You have made everything beautiful in its time. What's more, You have placed eternity in our hearts (Ecclesiastes 3:11), that we might respond with love, joy, and deep longing for the marvelous works of Your hands. Help me, to the best of my poor ability, to reflect Your loveliness in everything I do.

TO GOD BE THE GLORY

Therefore, whether you eat or drink, or
whatever you do, do all to the glory of God.
1 Corinthians 10:31, NKJV

Exhort bondservants to be obedient to their own
masters, to be well pleasing in all things, not answering
back, not pilfering, but showing all good fidelity, that they
may adorn the doctrine of God our Savior in all things.
Titus 2:9, 10, NKJV

If anyone speaks, let him speak as the oracles of God.
If anyone ministers, let him do it as with the ability
which God supplies, that in all things God may be
glorified through Jesus Christ, to whom belong the
glory and the dominion forever and ever. Amen.
1 Peter 4:11, NKJV

Like property and possessions, the biblical concept of *glory* is tied to the idea of personhood. *Glory* is an outward manifestation of a person's inner being. It emanates from within him, impacts his world, and returns to him again in the form of recognition or praise. In this sense, the idea of glory is

LABOR: created to **Create**

closely allied to that of work. The **work** we do says something about **who** we are and **whose** we are. If it is done well, it redounds, not only to **our** credit, but also to the honor of Him in whose image we are made.

As a Christian, have I considered how my work ethic reflects upon the God I claim to serve?

I realize, Father, that I am the only "Bible" some people will ever have an opportunity to "read." Help me, then, to do my work heartily, as unto You, that Your Truth may be enhanced in the eyes of those who have responsibility for my labor (Colossians 3:22, 23). As for those who are appointed to serve **me**, may I never forget to treat them with justice, fairness, and compassion. Remind me that my true Master is in heaven (Colossians 4:1) and enable me by my actions and attitudes to bring glory to Your name, that the world, in seeing me, may see You as You are.

COMPASSION AND PARTNERSHIP

"When you reap the harvest of your land, you shall
not wholly reap the corners of your field, nor shall
you gather the gleanings of your harvest. And you shall
not glean your vineyard, nor shall you gather every
grape of your vineyard; you shall leave them for the
poor and the stranger: I am the LORD your God."
Leviticus 19:9, 10, NKJV

Let him who stole steal no longer, but rather
let him labor, working with his hands what is good,
that he may have something to give him who has need.
Ephesians 4:28, NKJV

Come now, you rich, weep and howl for your miseries
that are coming upon you! ... Indeed the wages of the
laborers who mowed your fields, which you kept back
by fraud, cry out; and the cries of the reapers have
reached the ears of the Lord of Sabaoth.
James 5:1, 4, NKJV

God's concern for the poor is one of the most unremitting themes of the
entire Bible. Jesus said that an act of kindness extended to the needy

ultimately serves and honors **Him** (Matthew 25:40). But how do we begin to fulfill this urgent calling? The answer is rooted firmly in the sphere of **labor**. We work, not only to feed ourselves, but also in order to have something to **give**. And we give, not merely by donating a portion of our earnings to others, but also by granting them a share in the joy of productive labor.

To what extent do I view work, pay, and profit as the means of helping others?

God, You have told me again and again that my life does not consist in self-seeking but rather in loving You and serving other people (Matthew 16:25). I praise You for giving me the ability to produce material wealth (Deuteronomy 8:18) that can in turn be applied to the needs of the poor and hurting (James 2:15, 16). Help me to find practical ways of caring for those who lack, not merely food, shelter, and clothing, but also simple human dignity. Show me what I can do to draw them into the joy of creative and productive labor.

"Teacher, which is the greatest commandment in the Law?"

Jesus replied: " 'Love the Lord your God with all your heart

and with all your soul and with all your mind.'

This is the first and greatest commandment. And the second

is like it: 'Love your neighbor as yourself.' All the Law and the

Prophets hang on these two commandments."

Matthew 22:36-40 (NIV)

tour **12**

Community & Involvement

God cares. **Do I?**

"NOW I WILL ARISE"

"For the oppression of the poor, for the sighing
of the needy, now I will arise," says the LORD; "I will
set him in the safety for which he yearns."
Psalm 12:5, NKJV

"The Spirit of the LORD is upon Me, because He has
anointed Me to preach the gospel to the poor ..."
Luke 4:18, NKJV

Has God not chosen the poor of this world to be rich in
faith and heirs of the kingdom which He promised to those
who love Him? But you have dishonored the poor man ...
James 2:5, 6, NKJV

Does the Lord really look with special favor on the poor? Is there some
sense in which the gospel has been designed specifically with them in
mind? The Bible seems to say so. That's because God helps the helpless,
not those who imagine they can help themselves. To be without resource
or recourse is to know firsthand what it means to need a ***Savior***. And
to experience this need firsthand – to feel it from the heart – is to draw
another step closer to the One who delights to comfort and sustain.

Do I understand God's unique regard for the needy?

I realize, Lord, that I am poor and destitute – that, regardless of economic or social status, I desperately need Your mercy and Your grace. Thank You for directing Your thoughts toward me; You are my help and my deliverer (Psalm 40:17). Remind me constantly of the true nature of my condition, lest I be tempted to say, "I am rich, have become wealthy, and have need of nothing" (Revelation 3:17). Let me never forget the plight of those whose needs are even greater than my own.

GENTLE AND LOWLY IN HEART

Though the LORD is on high, yet He regards the lowly;
but the proud He knows from afar.
Psalm 138:6, NKJV

For thus says the High and Lofty One who inhabits
eternity, whose name is Holy: "I dwell in the high
and holy place, with him who has a contrite and
humble spirit, to revive the spirit of the humble, and
to revive the heart of the contrite ones."
Isaiah 57:15, NKJV

"Come to Me, all you who labor and are heavy
laden, and I will give you rest. Take My yoke upon
you and learn from Me, for I am gentle and lowly
in heart, and you will find rest for your souls."
Matthew 11:28, 29, NKJV

To see Christ is to see the Father (John 14:9). When the Lord Jesus tells us that He Himself is "gentle and humble in heart," He is in effect declaring that the universe turns upon a core of meekness, deference, and sincere regard for others. The all-powerful Creator does not simply look down with compassion upon the situation of the weak and marginalized; He enters into it and personally *identifies* with it. This remarkable message is unique among the philosophies and religions of the world.

Am I humble enough to identify with those who are hurting and needy?

_____

_____

_____

_____

_____

All praise, glory, and honor belong to You, O God. Great and mighty as You are, You do not scorn to draw near to the lowly. Your humility is evident in the courtesy and respect with which You treat the least of Your feeble and fainthearted creatures. It is not Your way to condescend. Instead, You make Yourself like one of us, preferring to demonstrate Your love by being gentle with the gentle and meek among the meek (Proverbs 16:19). Create in me a similar desire to cast my lot with the poor and disenfranchised.

"GO AND DO LIKEWISE"

[Jesus said,] "Which of these three do you think
was neighbor to him who fell among the thieves?"
And [the lawyer] said, "He who showed mercy on him."
Then Jesus said to him, "Go and do likewise."
Luke 10:36, 37, NKJV

...Do not set your mind on high things,
but associate with the humble.
Romans 12:16, NKJV

Pure and undefiled religion before God and the Father
is this: to visit orphans and widows in their trouble,
and to keep oneself unspotted from the world.
James 1:27, NKJV

"Who is my neighbor?" asked the teacher of the law. And Jesus responded,

"You're asking the wrong question. Definitions are not your concern. Your

task is to *be* a neighbor to all who require your help." God, says Jesus, is

love – *agape* love. And *agape* love is decisive and determined *action*. It's not enough to cultivate feelings of compassion for the needy. Instead, we must have the humility and courage to **reach out**. Only in this way can we become faithful imitators of our Lord and Master.

Am I willing to step outside my comfort zone in order to serve others?

_____

_____

_____

_____

_____

Father in heaven, I ask to be indwelt by the mind of Christ (1 Corinthians 2:16). Make me like Jesus, who did not consider equality with God a thing to be grasped, but humbled Himself, assuming the form of a servant and becoming obedient even to the point of death on a cross (Philippians 2:5-8). This He did for **my** sake and for the sake of **all** who are incapable of lifting their own heads above the tide of human trouble, toil, and woe. Give me strength to follow Him on the pathway of service to the least and the lost.

PHILANTHROPY AND CHARITY

So God created man in His own image; in the image of
God He created him; male and female He created them.
Genesis 1:27, NKJV

..."From the hand of every man's brother
I will require the life of man."
Genesis 9:5, NKJV

Have we not all one Father? Has not one God created us?
Malachi 2:10, NKJV

"Then the righteous will answer Him saying, 'Lord, when
did we see You hungry and feed You, or thirsty and give
You drink?' ... And the King will answer and say to them,
'Assuredly, I say to you, inasmuch as you did it to one of
the least of these My brethren, you did it to Me.'"
Matthew 25:37, 40, NKJV

"We live," wrote C. S. Lewis, in "a society of possible gods and goddesses."
"The dullest and most uninteresting person you talk to," he went on to
reflect, "may one day be a creature which, if you saw it now, you would

be strongly tempted to worship."[10] It's this eternal perspective that distinguishes Christian *charity (agape)* from secular *philanthropy*. To the genuine disciple of Jesus, the poor are not merely poor; they are, as Mother Teresa expressed it, "Christ in a distressing disguise."

Have I pondered the social implications of Creation and Incarnation?

_____

_____

_____

_____

Open the eyes of my heart, Lord. Help me to see Christ in the face of my brother. I speak not only of my fellow Christians, but of men, women, and children everywhere, believers and unbelievers alike. Rich or poor, black or white, Asian, European, or African, we all bear the eternal stamp of Your divine image. How can another man suffer and I remain untouched? Help me, then, as I have opportunity, to do good to all, especially to those who are of the household of faith (Galatians 6:10).

_____

[10] C. S. Lewis, *The Weight of Glory* (Grand Rapids, MI.: Wm. B. Eerdmans, 1972), 14-15.

TRANSFORMED TO TRANSFORM

Then the Spirit of the LORD came upon Jephthah,
and he passed through Gilead and Manasseh,
and passed through Mizpah of Gilead; and from Mizpah
of Gilead he advanced toward the people of Ammon.
Judges 11:29, NKJV

Then Zacchaeus stood and said to the Lord, "Look, Lord,
I give half of my goods to the poor; and if I have taken
anything from anyone by false accusation, I restore
fourfold." And Jesus said to him, "Today salvation has
come to this house, because he also is a son of Abraham."
Luke 19:8, 9, NKJV

Now when they saw the boldness of Peter and
John, and perceived that they were uneducated and
untrained men, they marveled. And they realized
that they had been with Jesus.
Acts 4:13, NKJV

True Christian charity and effective Christian action flow out of genuine
Christian *conversion* – a Christ-centered transformation of the heart. The
Lord's work can only be done only in the Lord's way; without the anointing

of the Holy Spirit, all our best efforts are only an empty show. He who is forgiven much loves much, and there is no telling how profoundly he may impact his world through the impetus of his love. But he who relies on his own resources will sooner or later find that the well runs dry.

Do I understand how deeply I am loved by God? Am I compelled by this knowledge to extend His love to others?

_____

_____

_____

_____

If anyone is in Christ, he is a new creation (2 Corinthians 5:17). This, O Lord, is Your promise to all who come to You by faith in the sacrifice of Your Son. Let this word become a dynamic, ever-present reality in my life. Create in me a clean heart, and renew a right spirit within me (Psalm 51:10). Fill me with **Your** Spirit and conform me day by day to the image of Christ, that, being transformed, I may go forth in the strength of Your power to uphold my brothers and teach transgressors Your ways (Luke 22:32; Psalm 51:13).

RISK AND CHANGE

For so it was, while Jezebel massacred the
prophets of the LORD, that Obadiah had taken one
hundred prophets and hidden them, fifty to a cave,
and had fed them with bread and water.
1 Kings 18:4, NKJV

And behold, a leper came and worshiped Him,
saying, "Lord, if You are willing, You can make me
clean." Then Jesus put out His hand and touched him,
saying, "I am willing; be cleansed." Immediately
his leprosy was cleansed.
Matthew 8:2, 3, NKJV

Greet Priscilla and Aquila, my fellow workers
in Christ Jesus, who risked their own necks
for my life, to whom not only I give thanks, but
also all the churches of the Gentiles.
Romans 16:3, 4, NKJV

It was death to defy Jezebel, but Obadiah risked it. The upshot? Prophecy
was preserved in Israel and seven thousand remained faithful to the Lord.
Priscilla and Aquila put their lives on the line for Paul; Paul's fearless

preaching took an empire by storm. Jesus dared to **touch** a leper and turned the world upside down. By the power of His love, we, too, can become agents of healing and transformation – but only to the extent that we're willing to cast aside comfort, security, and personal interest.

Do I understand what it means to take up the cross and put God's kingdom first?

_____

_____

_____

_____

For our sake, Lord Jesus, You endured the cross, despising the shame, that You might become the author and finisher of our faith (Hebrews 12:2). In every age of the church there have been men and women who were not afraid to follow Your courageous example—dedicated disciples who took no thought for their own lives (Matthew 6:25) but risked everything in hopes of drawing the hurting and needy into the circle of Your love. They loved the world with Your love, even though the world was not worthy of them (Hebrews 11:38). Make me a member of that faithful company.

"A FIRE IN MY BONES"

Then I said, "I will not make mention of Him,
nor speak anymore in His name." But His word was
in my heart like a burning fire shut up in my bones;
I was weary of holding it back, and I could not.
Jeremiah 20:9, NKJV

And some of the Pharisees called to Him from the
crowd, "Teacher, rebuke Your disciples." But He
answered and said to them, "I tell you that if these should
keep silent, the stones would immediately cry out."
Luke 19:39, 40, NKJV

But Peter and John answered and said to them,
"Whether it is right in the sight of God to listen to you
more than to God, you judge. For we cannot but speak
the things which we have seen and heard."
Acts 4:19, 20, NKJV

The truth will out, as the saying goes – and not merely in the sense that
the *real* story must eventually come to light. For ***God's*** Truth in the heart
is a living and active force. Like a pinch of yeast in a lump of dough, it
expands and grows until it finds an outlet. Truth possesses, constrains, and

compels. It is communicated, as Tolstoy says, from one soul to another, just as an endless number of candles are lighted from one. That light need only burn, and the darkness will melt like wax before the fire.

Do I grasp the power of the living Truth? Am I possessed by a vision of the glory of God in the face of Jesus Christ?

All praise, honor, and glory belong to You, eternal Lord. I Thank You that You have not left us ignorant of Your character, Your desires and expectations, or Your plan and purpose for our lives, but have revealed these things to us in terms we can understand. Your majesty is evident in the things You have made. Your words are set forth clearly in the pages of Scripture. In the person of Jesus Christ, You have walked among us, died for our deliverance, and risen again for our justification. How can I keep from singing the wonders of Your grace? How can I hide Your light beneath a bushel? Remove all restraint and let me burn like a torch for You. Make me a faithful witness of Your undying Truth.

Conclusion

ongratulations! You made it through all thirteen tours! During this course of study I hope you were also able to spend some time each day in communion with God, reflecting deeply and personally upon His wonderful truth claims. No doubt there were a lot of obstacles along the way. But then that's the nature of our walk. The road is seldom without distractions, obstructions, and even outright attempts on the part of the enemy to dissuade us from persevering.

Perhaps this is the first time you have made a consistent effort to commit yourself to daily prayer and meditation before the Lord. If so, I hope this has been just the beginning of a new phase in your life. I beg you to continue the good work you've begun. You have established a wonderful pattern. Hopefully, you have also experienced the blessed fruit of divine fellowship. Make it a forever habit!

You don't really need a guide, but if you find yourself floundering, there are a number of good ones available. With or without assistance, you can have confidence that the Word of God and the indwelling Holy Spirit will provide you with sufficient guidance for your own daily devotions. Spend time each day in the Scripture. Don't feel that you have to plow through a large section. Pray before you begin, asking God to reveal Himself to you through His Word. Then read a passage, a paragraph, a chapter, until you are struck by some aspect of God or His Truth. Stop and contemplate that Truth and be honest before God about what it reveals within you. It could be anything from ignorance to rebellion. Whatever it brings to light, confess that to the Lord and thank Him for who He is. I would also encourage you to journal your reflections, however briefly. It really does help bring clarity to your thinking.

God performed an interesting set of miracles while the children of Israel were trekking through the desert. The Scripture says that God kept their shoes and clothes from wearing out. He also kept their feet from swelling. Since He did all this, He could have miraculously kept them from needing food as well. But He didn't. Instead, He provided fresh bread every morning. The Israelites' responsibility was to go out and gather it daily. Storing yesterday's bread didn't work. Day-old manna always spoiled.

So, too, we need to feed upon Him *every day*. He provides the feast and stands knocking at the door of our hearts, waiting eagerly to dine with us. There is no handle on the outside of that door – *we* have to get up and open it for Him. *We* have to go out and pick up the manna every day. And when we do, the fellowship and communion we enjoy with Him beats the best seven-course meal ever prepared.

May you know His presence and the joy of walking with Him all the days of your life!

soli deo gloria!

DR. DEL TACKETT

is president of the Focus on the Family Institute® and senior vice president of Focus on the Family. He is also the architect and chief spokesperson for *Focus on the Family's The Truth Project*®—a nationwide initiative designed to bring the Christian worldview to the Body of Christ.

As a professor, Dr. Tackett has taught more than thirty undergraduate and graduate courses at three different institutions, and holds three earned degrees (D.M., Colorado Technical University; M.S., Auburn University; B.S., Kansas State University). He and his wife, Melissa, have four grown children and reside in Colorado Springs.

JIM WARE,

a graduate of UCLA and Fuller Theological Seminary, is the author of *God of the Fairy Tale* and co-author (with Kurt Bruner) of the best-selling *Finding God in the Lord of the Rings* and *Finding God in the Land of Narnia*. A Celtic music enthusiast, he enjoys playing the guitar and other stringed instruments with family and friends. He resides in Colorado Springs with his wife, Joni, and their six children.

But if I say, "I will not mention him or speak

any more in his name," his word is in my heart

like a fire, a fire shut up in my bones. I am weary

of holding it in; indeed, I cannot.

Jeremiah 20:9 (NIV)